New Path to Riches

How your neighbors are making a big second income by writing and publishing their own money-making websites.

Nick Usborne

Splinter Press
2009

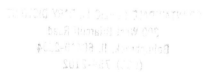

New Path
to Riches

How your neighbors are making a big
second income by writing and publishing
their own money-making websites.

Nick Usborne

TABLE OF CONTENTS

INTRODUCTION

Tens of thousands of people around the world, working in their spare time at home, are making thousands of dollars a month from websites they have created and written on topics that interest them.

And you can do the same. That's what this book is all about.

You'll learn about how changes in technology and in the publishing industry have opened the doors for gifted amateurs like yourself. You'll learn how to find niche topics about which people are hungry for quality information.

You don't need to be a professional writer. Nor do you need to be a qualified expert in the subject you write about. You just need to enjoy writing and be passionate about sharing information with others who are interested in the same topic.

The barriers to entry are minimal. It costs very little to build a website. And you won't have to pay for visitors to come to your site, because the new path to riches model I describe in this book is founded on having the search engines send you traffic for free.

Your job is simply to write authentic, engaging content for your site, and share it.

This book starts by explaining the changes that make this opportunity possible. You'll learn how big media has taken

1

a huge hit with the growth of the Internet, and how their struggles can be transformed into your opportunity.

You'll learn how to find the topics people are interested in, how to get listed high up in the search engines, how to promote your website and, of course, how to make some money.

Basically, you'll be writing about a subject that interests you, and you'll make money as a result. How much? Maybe $500 a month. Maybe $5,000 a month. Maybe even more. How much you make will depend on how well you choose your topic and how hard you work on your website.

But whether you make $500 or $5,000 a month, your own website could soon be earning you a very welcome second income.

It isn't difficult to do, but it does take some hard work and patience.

For me, the income I make from my own websites has made a big difference to my life. The money flows in every month, whether I'm sitting at my desk or not.

You can follow this new path to riches too.

Nick Usborne

NOTE: All the resources mentioned in this book can be found at NewPathToRiches.com.

CHAPTER ONE

JOIN YOUR NEIGHBORS IN WRITING MONEY-MAKING WEBSITES

Go to a few homes in your neighborhood and ask whoever opens the door whether he or she is making any money simply by writing online, and you may be surprised by how quickly you'll find someone who says yes.

The question itself would have been unthinkable twenty years ago. The fact that you will likely find someone who says yes, somewhere along your street, is remarkable.

Rapid changes in technology can make us a little blasé about some very fundamental changes that have been taking place in recent years. It's all too easy to take for granted that almost anything is possible through the Internet or via our mobile phones. Banking online? Of course. Choosing and booking vacations without leaving your home? No problem. Taking and sending photos with a cell phone? Why not? Reading the newspaper on your laptop? Makes sense.

But none of these things were possible twenty years ago.

High-tech changes are the ones that grab the headlines. But behind the drama, some profound shifts are taking place in a very established industry—publishing.

Publishing is no longer in the hands of the chosen few. Publishers and editors are no longer in control of the news. They are not even close in their second position. The primary disseminators of breaking news are people like you and me, armed with our cell phones, our blogs, and our Twitter accounts.

And it's not just the newspapers and TV stations which are taking a hit when it comes to news and publishing. Book publishers are hurting too. Fewer people are buying physical books.

Sure, some people now read books on their Kindles and other e-book readers. But there is something else happening. It is happening in a very, very big way. But we don't hear much about it. Big media companies, journalists, feature writers, and book authors are suddenly having to contend with a very large and determined group of competitors.

Who are these competitors? They are people like you and me.

The Web has democratized the process of writing and publishing.

For you and me to publish and share our knowledge, advice, and opinions, we no longer need a printing press, delivery trucks, or a store. We can write and publish online, often at no cost whatsoever.

Some will say that the democratization of writing has simply resulted in millions of pages of low-quality rubbish being published online.

For sure, there is low quality and pretty useless and uninteresting stuff being published. But to dismiss every "writer next door" simply because there is a lot of rubbish out there is a very defensive posture to take. It's a patriarchal attitude, suggesting that for writing to have value it first has to go through an editor and publisher.

I don't think so.

Publishers of books, newspapers, and magazines would love to have us believe that *they* are the only reliable arbiters of quality writing and information. That has been their position and the foundation of their businesses for about five hundred years now. If you wanted to get published you first had to be judged worthy by a professional editor.

Sorry Mr. Editor. But those days are past. And you know it. You also know that you have published some rubbish of your own over the years.

There are tens of thousands of quality "writers next door." They write and publish remarkable websites and blogs. They are functioning totally outside of the traditional world of publishing. They aren't printing their work on paper and don't need anyone's approval or permission to publish or distribute what they write.

The days of dead-tree publishing and having to get "approval" to publish are behind us.

People are writing online about every topic under the sun.

One of the things that changes when you become your own editor and publisher online is that you are able to address much narrower segments than traditional publishers. We'll look at this in more detail later on. For now, it suffices to say that while scales of economy prevent big publishers from launching books and magazine on tightly-niched topics, writers who publish online don't have that problem.

Online you can become the author of a site on very specific and narrow topics, like organic household cleaning, pet stores in Manhattan, or vegetarian couscous recipes. Online your audience is global, and you don't have to ship atoms (books) from one part of the country to another, or to other countries.

The fact that a website can be found and accessed from any part of the world, at no extra cost to you, changes everything. Access to a global audience is just one of the things that make it possible for your neighbor to become a successful online publisher.

So how about you? Is there a topic that interests you? Remember, you don't need to be an expert. You don't need to be a professional on your topic. You just have to be able to write, and have a subject you would like to write about.

To put all this into context, take a look at one of my own websites, CoffeeDetective.com.

I am not a coffee professional. I have never worked in the coffee industry. Nor have I taken any courses about making coffee. But I do like coffee and am interested in many aspects of coffee and coffee making.

A few years ago I decided to get started and created the site with maybe fifteen pages in total. Today it has over 700 pages and is growing day by day. And now I don't even have to write all the pages myself. My readers submit their own coffee reviews, photos, questions, and comments.

If you can, spend a little time on that site and see what I have done.

It's not a very sophisticated website. It doesn't look terribly slick or professional. And that's because I haven't spent much money on its design or functionality. It is just a place where I can write about various aspects of making and enjoying gourmet coffee at home.

You'll also notice from my writing on the site that I don't sound like an industry expert on the topic. I'm just a guy who knows more about coffee than my neighbors. We'll look at this more in Chapter Three, because the rise of the "expert next door" is having a profound impact on what gets read.

Right now that site attracts over a thousand visitors a day. They almost all arrive through search engines like Google and Bing. I don't pay for that traffic. I simply write pages that are useful enough for people to want to read and share.

My site is one of tens of thousands of "writer next door" websites. All are written by passionate amateurs. None have been approved or even seen by traditional publishers.

Could you do the same? Yes, you almost certainly can. You're probably already writing online. Maybe you add comments to your favorite blogs. Or you have a Twitter account or Facebook page.

You already know how simple it is to communicate online with others who share the same interests.

The step to actually creating a website of your own and filling it with interesting, quality information is a very small one.

If this is the new path to riches, how can *you* make money by writing a website or a blog?

Not everyone who writes online makes money or even wants to make money. Some people are very happy to contribute their opinions and expertise just for the raw pleasure of it. Consider Wikipedia. Wikipedia is an online encyclopedia, published in multiple languages and all written by gifted, passionate amateurs. None of the writers are paid for their work. Why do they put in so much time without any prospect of being paid? Because they enjoy what they do. Because they feel they are making a worthwhile contribution.

But if you do want to make some money in return for your efforts, there are certainly ways to do that. As the publisher of your own website or websites you can put yourself in the position of an intermediary. To put it another way, you will grow an audience that companies would like to sell stuff to. That gives your site value.

Take another look at some of the pages at CoffeeDetective.com. You'll see that many of them include text ads delivered by Google. I just put some code on the page and Google delivers ads which are paid for by companies which would like to sell stuff to my audience of coffee lovers. If someone clicks on one of those ads, the advertiser is billed for the click, and Google and I share the revenue.

You will also see a lot of links on those pages. Some of the links point at other pages on the site, while others point to outside websites. Many of those external links send my readers to sites which sell coffee and coffee makers. I don't get paid for the click, as I do with the Google ads, but I do get a commission if that click results in a sale. This is called affiliate marketing and is an excellent way for people to monetize their websites.

I also occasionally run ads for coffee companies which approach me directly. They want to reach my readers and they pay to have their advertisement included on some of my pages.

Finally, if you find my coffee page for beginners, you will see that I also sell an inexpensive e-book to help people who are just starting out in their love affair with gourmet coffee. When people buy that guide, I get the revenue.

These are just four of the ways you can make money by becoming an online publisher. One way or another, as soon as you have an audience, you have the potential to generate an ongoing stream of income.

Interestingly, these same revenue sources are also used by some of the largest content sites on the Web. Go to CNN or NewYorkTimes.com and you'll find both display ads (banners) and some contextual text ads.

Whether it's The New York Times, me with my coffee site, or you with your own site, we are all on a level playing field. We all have the same possibilities when it comes to making money. The scale is somewhat different, but the revenue model is the same.

Think about that. The Web actually enables you to launch a business with the exact same business model as some of the largest publishing companies out there. In fact, as we will see later, you can sometimes beat them at their own game. Best of all, unlike in the world of bricks and mortar, the price of admission is almost negligible. You can set up your website for about the same price as breakfast for two at McDonalds.

As one person working from home you don't have to worry about paying salaries, buying printing presses, or leasing a fleet of trucks to deliver newspapers, magazines or books. Your total costs will comprise a very modest website hosting fee, and the time you choose to spend writing.

Why income from your own websites is the best kind of income to have.

For most of my adult life I have earned my living as a freelance copywriter, first in the world of print and then, for the last 10 years, online. It has been a rewarding career for me. But for all that time, I made money only when I was working. More or less, I was paid for the hours I worked, and wasn't paid for the time I wasn't working.

This was fine most of the time, but it made me think twice about taking long vacations. If I was away from my desk for two or three weeks, that was two or three weeks when I wasn't earning a penny.

This is pretty much the case for most of us. If you are an employee, even while you might get paid vacations, for most of the year you are paid on the understanding that you will turn up for work and put in a certain number of hours each week.

If you are a lawyer or consultant the same holds true. You watch the hours as an indicator of how much you are going to earn.

But money coming in from a website such as mine is known as "passive income." Once you build up a body of visitors and they start clicking on money-making links, you'll make money whether you are at your desk or not.

Recently I took a two week vacation and didn't take my laptop. Nor did I access any computers while I was away. During that period, there was a certain drop in some areas of my income, as there are some things I do which still require me to be sitting at my desk and working.

But over that two-week period there was no change in the income from my CoffeeDetective.com website. I was relaxing, enjoying myself, and staying away from computers, but was still making money. But what if I had spent more than two weeks away from my desk? Last year I got so busy with other work, I didn't find time to work on my coffee site at all for about three months. Again, there was no decline in my income. The dollars kept coming in at the same rate.

I don't want to make a habit of ignoring my site, and usually spend two or three hours a week editing pages, adding new pages, and finding ways to improve the overall experience on the site. I want the site to grow, to become better. I want more and more visitors. I want my income to increase. But I can do this work as and when I feel like it. There are no deadlines. I don't have a boss or a client. And if I do need to ignore the site for a few weeks or even months, I can do so without any ill effects.

This is pretty remarkable. Many of us grew up with a work ethic that told us we would make an honest day's wage for an honest day's work. There is something of the Puritan in this. To be a good person you have to work hard for your money. And you make money only when you roll up your sleeves and are actually working.

The exception, of course, has always been that business owners can make money at any time of the day by employing other people to do the actual labor for them. Successful business people have always been able to enjoy a passive income. That said, the idea of being a business owner and spending your time on the golf course is something of a myth. Most employers will tell you they have to put in more work than the people they employ.

Or, if you have millions of dollars in hand you can invest them and enjoy a passive income from the interest that money earns.

However, most of us are not employers, nor do we have millions of spare dollars to invest.

What the Web is doing right now is enabling regular people to earn a significant passive income in their spare time. Working on your own, investing a few hours a week, you can now join the exclusive club of those who earn a passive income.

It is tempting to take this for granted, as just another of the benefits of being on the Web. But to do so is to minimize both the opportunity and the enormity of the shift that is taking place. As we will see in the next chapter, the changes taking place in the world of publishing right now are not gentle, they are tectonic. The traditional publishing industry, which has remained largely unchanged for hundreds of years, is showing some massive cracks in its structure.

Do you have to be a professional writer in order to make money from your own websites?

Absolutely not. Of all the people I know who make money by writing their own websites, only a very few have any professional background in writing. Most are just regular people who have the normal writing skills one picks up in everyday life. They write e-mails to friends and relatives. They write comments on blogs. They just enjoy using the written word to share what they know and express their opinions.

Again, this is an extraordinary shift from traditional ways of making money as a writer. Until now it has almost been a given that to make money by writing one has to study hard, take exams, and end up with a degree or some other professionally recognized qualification.

But making money by writing your own websites takes you outside of that traditional structure. The act of writing, publishing, and making money from your efforts has become democratized in a massive way.

In other words, this opportunity is open to anyone and everyone. You don't need any training, certificate, or recognized qualifications. You just need to write in a way that comes naturally to you.

The door is wide open (wider than you think), but not many people know it.

Technology news always focuses on what's happening now, the leading edge. We hear about the latest gadgets, the newest operating systems, the thinnest laptops, the latest micro-blogging platform and so on.

But for our purposes the really interesting stuff is actually happening well back from the leading edge.

New technologies, services, and tools tend to follow the usual bell curve. First the early adopters try something new. Their numbers are small, but their enthusiasm and influence is significant. These early adopters are followed by a larger group of slightly less adventurous people who are interested in trying something once it has received the thumbs-up from the early adopters. Finally, the masses come on board. It happens in fashion. It happens in consumer electronics, such as with iPods and plasma TVs. And it happened with the Internet.

As I write this, there are now over one billion people around the world accessing the Internet. That represents 16% of the total population of the world. In other words, what was once leading edge technology now has mass appeal.

One billion people want to find answers online. In addition to the e-mails they send, the games they play, the sports results they follow, and the conversations they have, they also want to know stuff. Find out about stuff.

They want to know where the best beaches are in Kenya, which coffee has the most caffeine, how to keep squirrels out of bird feeders, how to mend a wrist watch, where to buy roses, how to cook a great dinner for two for under

$5, how to play poker, where to find out what brand of sunglasses Michael Jackson wore.

Across the major search engines there are several billion searches made each and every day. That's billions, not millions. It is within this mass of global searching that our opportunity lies.

Forget the leading edge, unless you are a software genius or have a ton of money. For the rest of us, there is an extraordinary opportunity to be found in that vast volume of everyday searches.

And that opportunity is wide open for a very important reason.

Large publishers of online content don't do a very good job of answering questions like, "How do I keep squirrels out of my bird feeder?" Large media groups focus primarily on the dissemination of news (preferably disasters or political scandals), celebrity gossip, sports, and other areas where they know that millions of people will be interested. Their revenue model demands that they publish information on topics which have broad appeal across the population.

While the large online media groups take care of the big, popular topics like Hollywood and the Super Bowl, who is going to answer those billions of questions about much narrower topics?

The answer to that is...you are. It is people like you who write and publish useful and interesting information about narrower, special-interest topics.

Let's go back to the question about those pesky squirrels. Without the Internet, how would you find an answer to that question? Not from your local or national newspaper. Probably not from a magazine rack, unless you were very lucky and found the one issue of the last decade that actually had an article on the topic. Not from a book, unless you scanned the table of contents of dozens of books about birds and gardens. And even then you might miss the one paragraph that was relevant.

Without the Internet, the most likely source of that information would probably be a relative, friend, or neighbor. You ask the people you know. And you would pick those people who had gardens with bird-feeders. That said, because of the limits on the number of people you know with bird feeders, you would be lucky to get the answer you want.

But what if you had immediate access to millions of "neighbors" who have bird feeders? What if you could ask them all, simultaneously? Or what if you could ask Google to find the answer for you?

All this is to point out that there are millions of unanswered questions out there. And in many cases, the answers are not being found.

As an example, let's take another look at my coffee site, CoffeeDetective.com. I offer a Q&A service on the site.

My readers use a form to send in questions, and I provide the answers.

Here is a list of the kind of questions I receive.

What proportion of coffee to water should I use?

Where can I find an all-metal or all-glass coffee maker?

Does dark roasted coffee stain your teeth more?

Why doesn't Dunkin Donut coffee taste the same at home?

Should I store my coffee beans in the fridge?

Is coffee good for plants?

Are chemicals used to make flavored coffee?

Is there a drip coffee maker with no plastic parts?

How do you make Swedish coffee?

Is coffee fattening?

Paper vs. metal coffee filters. Which is best?

Do you think you could find the answers to those questions in your local library? Or in a magazine or on TV? Almost certainly not. In fact, without the Internet you would be very lucky to be able to find answers to those questions anywhere.

The same kinds of questions are being asked about every topic under the sun, every minute of every day.

These are the types of question that big media are very ill-suited to answer. It just doesn't fit with their business model.

But when you, as an individual, pick a topic about which you are already reasonably knowledgeable, you are in the perfect position to create a website that addresses these very specific questions.

Therein lies the opportunity for gifted amateurs, the experts next door...you and me.

CHAPTER TWO

OUT WITH OLD PUBLISHING, IN WITH THE NEW

What we are witnessing today is the most dramatic fragmentation of the publishing industry to occur within the last 500 years. And when established industries fall apart, something has to rise out of the ashes. Both nature and business abhor a vacuum. As traditional publishing falls apart, a vacuum is being created. People still want to know the news, and they still want to find out how to get hold of a squirrel-proof bird feeder.

We used to be slaves to big media. We would watch their programs on TV, we would buy their magazines and we would read their books. But throughout that experience we would learn only what they decided we *should* learn. They would cover only those topics which they felt would draw the biggest audiences or sell the most copies of their magazines or books.

When it came to smaller, niche topics, old media didn't address our individual needs, because to do so didn't fit with the economies of scale they depended on.

The Web has turned that math upside down. With the Web it is the reader who is in control and the reader who decides what information they want.

Old, traditional media have lost control.

Old media can no longer determine what it is I should learn about gardening, for example. Their editors can no longer decide which gardening tips I should receive in the spring.

By going to a search engine like Google, it is the reader who becomes the arbiter of what he or she wants to know about. There may be nothing in any major publications this week about organic slug control. But I can decide to find out about exactly that, simply by doing a search for *organic slug control* in a search engine. And I can decide to do it at the time of my own choosing.

The simple act of an individual going to Google and deciding for him or herself exactly what it is he or she would like to find changes everything.

As we will see in later chapters, your task as a writer at home is simply to identify the niche subject topics people are interested in, but which aren't being adequately addressed by larger publishers.

You'll be "finding the gap."

Old media is struggling with the fragmentation of attention.

The Web has also changed the way in which people spend their time. Fewer and fewer people are devoting hours on end to reading a single newspaper or book. Our attention is being fragmented in ways that were never possible just a few years ago.

Take a look at a friend or family member when they are online. Their attention skips from e-mails to websites to social media platforms at an incredible speed. We are becoming self-directed browsers of information, having a taste of a little bit of everything. During the course of a session online we might access our favorite news site, then skip over to YouTube to watch a three-minute video, then quickly open our Twitter page, then post a photo to our Facebook page, and maybe add it to our Flickr page. After that we may play an online game, chat with friends through instant messaging, and then get interrupted by someone sending us a text message or photo on our cell phone.

We are no longer persuaded that the best and most interesting use of our time is to sit in front of the TV and watch a 60-minute documentary on CBS, interrupted by inane advertisements. We would rather make our own choices and apply micro-attention to a very broad range of topics and services online.

Big media has a huge problem with micro-attention. Its business model simply can't accommodate it. In particular, that business model can't survive within an environment in which the reader or viewer is in control and making his or her own choices about what to do, what to see, what to read, and how much time to remain engaged.

Say hello to new publishing.

The Web has changed more than just the ability of someone to write something and upload it to a blog or a website. The Web has spawned a huge range of different publishing platforms, each of them designed to allow writers to bypass the old ways, ignore the gatekeepers and middlemen, and take control of the entire publishing process.

Take this book for instance. It wasn't published through a traditional publisher. I have taken that route in the past and the outcome was that my publisher never bothered to put much effort into marketing the book, so I never made much of an income from it. Essentially, they simply provided proofing, printing, and distribution services.

I no longer need a big New York publisher to do that for me. Instead, I worked with Splinter Press, which is an imprint of the POD service company BookLocker.com. They took care of the design, layout, and printing of the book for me. Plus they handled and continue to handle distribution to online stores like Amazon.

Between them, BookLocker and Amazon do everything my old publisher did. And the proportion of revenues I receive is about three times as much.

You can do the same. Anyone can. We don't need traditional publishers any more. When we do use them, the lion's share of revenues goes to covering their vast, archaic overhead structure.

Or maybe you would prefer to publish and distribute your own print magazine. No problem. Check out MagCloud.com. If you are not interested in creating a physical book or magazine, publish your work as an e-book and list it at eBooks.com.

Or perhaps you would simply like to make your books, reports, reviews, or articles available for free, and not even want a website of your own. Go to Scribd.com. If you want to make TV shows or your own radio show, you can do those online too.

It's little wonder that traditional publishers are shaking in their boots and wondering what's coming next.

As a writer you now have a wide array of platforms to use. You can publish your work for sale, or give it away free. Either way, the Web is an extraordinary enabler. It does away with the middlemen, it removes the gatekeepers, it takes an industry that survived on top-down control and puts control directly into the hands of readers and writers.

Welcome to a world where failure doesn't cost much.

When a book is printed by a traditional publisher, huge amounts of resources and money go into the production and distribution of that physical book. If sales are disappointing, the cost of that failure is significant.

Not so when you publish through the Web. When it comes to publishing through a website or blog, the costs are either zero or very close. So if you do pick a topic for a website and then discover, six months later, that not enough people are interested in what you are writing, just pull the plug. You will have lost some time, but not much money.

The low cost of failure means that as writers we can experiment. It also gives us a huge advantage over larger media companies. Large media companies have to do some scary math, make sure there is a large audience ready and waiting for them, and hope they can attract enough advertisers to fill the coffers. The cost of failure is big, and that creates a work environment based on caution. The result, as we see on our TV screens and in newspapers and magazines, is mediocrity. Taking the safe path means taking the boring path. Risk becomes a dirty word.

A culture based on risk-aversion holds you back. But when you take the opposite path, and embrace risk, your chances of creating something both remarkable and welcome increase exponentially.

Consider the cost of publishing your own website.

- Domain name, per year, less than $10.

- Website hosting. Between free and $20 a month, depending on the service you use and the functionality you want included.

Your top-end price for being an online publisher with your own website is $250 a year. If that sounds too rich for you, you can always publish your writing through a free blog service like Blogger.com or WordPress.org. Either way, thanks to the Web, you can now make money by writing online at almost no cost and no risk.

Are you beginning to see the gap, and the opportunity?

Traditional publishers, both offline and online, focus on the big topics, because they need a big audience to make money.

Traditional publishers are risk-averse and cautious about trying anything new.

Traditional publishers are hobbled by their huge cost structures. They can't risk focusing on micro-topics.

Traditional publishers are losing advertising dollars hand-over-fist as companies move their marketing dollars online.

Traditional publishers are rarely passionate.

Traditional publishers are very slow to act and execute.

In an article for the New York Times, journalist David Carr wrote recently about a huge launch party, 10 years ago, for the now defunct magazine, Talk.

Here is just one paragraph from that article:

> "Too bad nobody saw the sharks circling in the harbor. Rather than the culmination of a century of press power, the Talk party was the end of an era, a

literal fin de siècle. Flush with cash from the go-go '90s and engorged by spending from the dot-com era, mainstream media companies seemed poised on the brink of something extraordinary. But that brink ended up being a cliff."

One other thing that is killing all big media is that they no longer know how to talk to their readers.

For hundreds of years we became used to the idea of getting the information we needed from qualified experts.

We just assumed that an article which had passed through the hands of a professional editor was better than one that had not.

If we wanted to get reliable information about some arcane topic, we looked it up in Encylopedia Britannica and felt reassured when it turned out the entry had been penned by a Nobel Prize winner.

If we needed insights into how we could improve our business, we were likely to ask someone with an MBA.

This attitude to learning and exploring our world in general had almost become embedded into our DNA. If the author didn't have the correct job title or letters after his or her name, then we took the information with a pinch of salt.

Traditional publishers knew this and took advantage of it. They presented themselves as the experts, the arbiters of quality information. They gave us only the information they chose to select, but at least they gave us what was perceived as being reliable information. The publishers and editors were in control and we looked up to them as trusted patriarchs.

That has now changed. We may not think much about it, but the Web generation is far less impressed with a PhD than it was 10 years ago. We are no longer looking just for information that has a formal stamp of approval. Our taste in information has changed. We are more likely to turn to Wikipedia than to Encyclopedia Britannica.

Let's take a closer look at Wikipedia, because it illustrates very well how things have been changing.

As you probably know, Wikipedia is open to everyone. You can go to the site right now and change the entry it has for J.F. Kennedy. If you want, and I'm not encouraging you to do so, you can change the entry to say he was born in Iceland. A wiki is a site that enables any visitor to make editorial additions and changes to the site. You can do it from within your browser. There is no boss. No editor in chief. No filter. Not even an approval process.

You might think this means that Wikipedia entries are hopelessly inaccurate. That is a reasonable assumption because we have been raised during an era in which we were taught that only qualified experts in positions of authority could provide us with trustworthy answers.

Interestingly, the assumption that the removal of the gatekeeper will result in lower quality and more errors is incorrect. Wikipedia is remarkably accurate. And if you did write that JFK was born in Iceland you would find that your edit would be very quickly corrected, often within a matter of minutes.

Wikipedia has a number of things in its favor. First, if an error creeps in, Wikipedia self-heals very, very quickly. The knowledge of the masses is vast, and it is applied quickly. However, with Encyclopedia Britannica an error can be corrected only when the next edition is published and printed.

Second, Wikipedia has many, many more entries than Encyclopedia Britannica. This is made possible by the fact that there is no limit to the number of "volumes" one can print, nor any printing costs associated with the total number of entries. When you take out the cost of cutting down and processing dead trees, there really is no need to limit the number of entries.

This again points to the fundamental difference between old media and new media. With Encyclopedia Britannica there are editors who decide which information should be included and which information isn't important or interesting enough. New media doesn't draw that line. Even if an entry is interesting to a total of five people globally, one of those five can write the entry for Wikipedia. The other four can then read, edit and add to it.

This movement from trusting the writing of experts only to trusting the information created by the expert next door is having a profound impact. And the wider the door opens for people like you and me to share our knowledge, insights, and opinions, the greater the opportunity we have to make money from what we write online.

Quite apart from the impact of the growth of the Web, big media has been doing a great job of shooting itself in the foot.

The news media has not been doing a very good job of building our trust.

The concept of the media as the Fifth Estate was once central to its authority. We trusted national TV news, newspapers, and magazines because we felt we could rely on them to dig deep and expose the truth.

A prime example of this was when the Washington Post wrote about Watergate and was ultimately instrumental in the fall of Richard Nixon. That's the kind of thing we wanted the media to do. They were our eyes and ears, our conscience and our sword.

Fast forward to the run-up to the last Iraq war and you see the media playing a very different role. Where were the tough editorials? Where were the investigative reporters? Big media no longer seems to be there for us when we want tough questions asked and answered.

It is little wonder that online new sources, outside of big media, have been growing in popularity.

These multiple threads combine to put the power of writing into YOUR hands.

You might well be thinking this chapter points to a legitimate change in how the Web generation looks for and finds information, but still can't accept that you could become a profitable writer online yourself.

Maybe you think you're not smart enough. Maybe you believe that there is nothing you know enough about.

But the thing most likely to be holding you back is that you are still attached to the old paradigm that says you have to be an accredited professional in order to presume you are worthy to be published.

It can be tough to break out of that mindset.

But as I have mentioned, I have no professional background in coffee, but still have a website on that topic. Ellen Ferlazzo, who also writes a website part-time, isn't a food scientist, but she still writes about low-cost meals on her site CheapCooking.com.

Remember, when people look for information on the Web, they are no longer filtering results and knowledge based on the formal qualifications of the writer. The Web has changed that.

CHAPTER THREE

THE METEORIC RISE OF
THE EXPERT NEXT DOOR

Here's something else big media doesn't get. They don't get that the Web has changed the way in which people interact. We no longer all line up facing the TV or reading the day's top headlines. We have turned. We have turned to face one another. We now spend less and less time facing towards big media and more and more time facing each another.

Hundreds of millions of people interact via blogs, instant messaging, MySpace, Facebook, Twitter, and elsewhere. These websites are not in the business of publishing, they are in the business of enabling people to communicate with one another.

If I have a passion for repairing old wrist watches, I will soon find communities and groups which share my interest. I will find others like myself. Never mind that some of us are in North America, some are in Russia, and some are in New Zealand. We all get together and share what we know.

If I want to know how to take the movement out of a Girard Perregaux watch, it probably won't take me long to find someone who can help me. How else could I learn that?

As you are reading this page, millions upon millions of people are sharing what they know, feel, and believe. This scale of one-to-one communication has never before been possible.

As this happens, minute by minute, two things are happening.

First, people are picking up new communications skills. Adults, who may have written barely anything since leaving high school, are learning a whole new way of writing. They may be commenting on a blog post and writing a hundred words. Or they may be writing a Tweet for Twitter, with a maximum of 140 characters. But they are writing. They are asking questions and providing answers. They are sharing their knowledge and becoming better and better at expressing themselves, day by day. We are becoming a world of proficient writers, albeit in a different way.

Second, people are developing a preference for learning not from experts, but from others like themselves. They are picking up new knowledge from the expert next door, even if that person is only virtually next door.

As an example, let's say you want to figure out why the roses in your garden are not blooming. And let's say your neighbor has outstanding roses. What would you do? Would you try to find a professional gardener, or would you just ask your neighbor? So long as you are on good speaking terms, it would probably be easiest just to lean over the garden fence and ask him for his advice.

What the Web does is expand the concept of the expert next door. They no longer need to be next door. They could be in South Africa or South Korea. It doesn't matter. When you are on the Web, distance is no longer a factor. Geography becomes irrelevant.

Information from the expert next door is good enough.

The Web has fundamentally changed what we want when we consume products, services and information.

The sound quality of MP3 recordings is poor when compared to a CD. But it's good enough when we consider the convenience of downloading songs to our iPods.

The video quality on YouTube is terrible when compared to high definition movies, but it's good enough when we want to watch a 3-minute clip.

The video quality of a Flip Ultra camcorder is not very good when compared to more sophisticated models, but it's good enough for when we want to take a video of our kid's birthday party. It's a lot less expensive than other models as well.

A netbook computer doesn't have the speed and memory of a full-sized laptop, but it's good enough for surfing the Web, answering email and writing articles or web pages.

It's the same with asking our neighbor about roses. He may not be a qualified expert, but his expertise is good enough to help us.

You don't have to stress about peak quality when you write your own website. You just have to make the information good enough to meet the immediate needs of your readers.

It's also a matter of trust.

While we may not view the information from our virtual neighbor as always being 100% accurate, we do trust these people to have good intentions and to be sincere. Yes, there will be some bad apples in the barrel. But generally people are generous with the information they share. As Wikipedia demonstrates, there are many people out there who are happy to invest time and energy in sharing what they know. They do it sincerely and with the intention of being helpful.

It's the fact that this information is shared openly, and not for some kind of payment, that makes us feel more comfortable. When we hear from a politician, we know he or she has a hidden agenda at play. His or her answer will be tainted by his or her own goals and motivations. The same is true when we hear from a company or an individual marketer. We can't be sure whether the answer to a question is serving our best interests or theirs. Although we suspect the latter.

The same goes for our question about our sickly roses. If we ask a professional and he says we should dig our roses up and he can come around and replace them with a better variety, what are we to think? Is his advice sincere, or is he trying to sell us some roses? We don't have that same problem when listening to the advice of our neighbor, the expert next door. We can assume that his advice will be untainted.

Our mistrust of politicians, companies, lawyers, and even medical professionals is growing. And they have only themselves to blame.

It is little wonder that communication platforms online are being crowded with millions of people who would rather learn from each other.

When we look at the opportunity presented by writing your own website, the issue of trust is key. A successful money-making website presents itself not as a professional source of information, but as the expert next door. The idea is to fill the gap left by people's growing mistrust of professionals.

A website that is created by the expert next door also does a much better job of tapping into all the social networking platforms you will find online. When you see a company logo as the avatar on a Twitter account, you quite correctly ask yourself, "What's their game? What do they want me to do? What are they trying to sell me?" And, of course, they are trying to sell you something. That's their job. Put simply, companies don't belong on social networks. It's not their place. They are there only because it allows them to reach a large audience of prospective customers. They are there to do business. If you are a real person and you have a website rich in useful and helpful information, you do belong on Twitter, and you would do well to use a headshot of yourself as your avatar. Social media sites are a natural home for the expert next door.

But there is one caveat. *To belong on social media platforms you have to be writing your website with the primary purpose of helping others.* If your primary purpose is simply to sell stuff, then your motivations will be no different from those of a regular company. Your readers will figure this out pretty quickly and they will no longer trust you.

And no, neither you nor a large company can get by this simply by writing a tagline that says something like, "Your trusted source in rose care." Trust is not a factor of what you say, it's the outcome of who you are and what you do.

We all look for a sense of local community.

In the Western world, most of our local communities are dead or dying. The local stores are gone, the local post office is gone, the small community meeting hall is gone. These days we barely know our neighbors and, as soon as we get to know the manager at a local store, either the manager moves on or the store closes.

But we still like to feel we are part of a community of individuals. The gap created by the loss of local community is now being filled by online websites, blogs, forums, and social media sites.

The geography of our social groups has changed, but we are still able to connect with real people who share our interests and concerns.

Again, your job as the writer of a money-making website is to join the relevant communities and to be generous in the information you share. How are you going to make money just by being a good friend to others? We'll get to that. It's a key question and, fortunately, there are some very good answers.

The power of aggregated knowledge and wisdom.

The factors that allow Wikipedia to be a trusted source of information also enable the expert next door to become a reliable source of knowledge. In Wikipedia you can feel confident about the accuracy of a page simply because while it wasn't written by a Nobel laureate, it was written and edited by dozens of informed people. If someone makes a mistake, another person corrects it. If new information comes to light, someone adds it. Instead of relying on the knowledge of an individual expert, it depends on the aggregated knowledge of a lot of gifted amateurs. And the process works well.

Let me give you an example from my coffee site. On CoffeeDetective.com I answer questions. Someone might write in and ask me if there are any coffee makers out there that are free of plastic parts. Interesting question, I do a little research and then write an answer. But that's not the end of it, because each Q&A page also has a comments function. So other people chip in with their own comments, and might identify some other plastic-free coffee makers that I missed. Others might make the point that not all plastics are equally evil when it comes to one's health.

In short, I am tapping into the aggregate wisdom of the crowd.

Just as important, by opening my site up to comments in this way, I am saying something to all of my readers. I am saying, "Hey, I may be the expert next door, but I don't know absolutely everything there is to know about coffee and coffee makers. If you have something to contribute, please share."

That's the different between an expert next door and a professional expert with letters after his name. The expert next door is open to discussion and happy to share the credit for a question well answered.

Empathy – hello right brain, goodbye left brain.

The left side of your brain is the analytical side. It does math for you. The right side of your brain sees the beauty in a painting or a piece of music.

Since the beginning of the Age of Enlightenment in eighteenth century Europe, the act of scientific reasoning has been held as the only reliable source of authority and legitimacy. That is why here in the Western World our approach to medicine and healing is a left-brain affair. We find answers through a process of careful scientific discovery. Not so in the Far East, where treatments are much more of a right-brain process.

In many ways Westerners have been prisoners of this approach to answering questions and making discoveries. For someone to have legitimacy and authority, they have to be a professional with the proper qualifications.

This had impacted our approach to science, government, business, and publishing.

But that is changing. We are slowly discovering the value of right-brain thinking. Right brain thinkers have more empathy and are more likely to make intuitive leaps. In some professions the value of empathetic thinking is well recognized. Nurses, for instance, are at their best when they not only have the correct training, but also show great empathy to their patients.

What is empathy? It is the genuine ability to feel what another person is feeling, to live inside his skin, to walk in his shoes.

And it is not just in the caring professions that the recognition of the power of empathy is growing. Many businesses are now putting increasing emphasis on an employee's ability to empathize with others. If you went for a job interview twenty years ago, the discussion would be all about your qualifications and training. Today you might go to an interview and not even be asked to show your college graduation certificate. But you will be asked a lot of questions designed to determine how empathetic you are. The interviewer wants to know how well you will work with others, and how effectively you will truly understand what is happening within the lives and work days of your colleagues.

Empathy is a tricky skill to learn. Those who have it have generally always had it. It's almost a character trait. When people pretend to be empathetic, you can usually tell that it's not genuine. I had a boss once who was convinced he was endowed with more than his fair share of empathy. But he wasn't. What he did was to go through the motions and ask all the right questions. He expressed great concern about how everyone in the company was feeling. But he didn't get it at all. He was almost totally blind to the feelings of the people he worked with.

What's the big deal? The big deal is that the Web has opened the door to the rise of empathy and its availability.

Sticking with the medical theme, imagine you have recently been diagnosed with cancer. Your doctor is sympathetic and doing all that he can. Your family is in shock. They love you, but don't really understand what you are going through. But you urgently feel the need for true empathy. You want to know you are not alone. You need to be among people who know exactly how you are feeling. What do you do? You go online.

There are dozens of websites, e-mail groups, forums, and communities online for people with cancer. Again, geography evaporates. Wealth and social standing fall by the wayside. It doesn't matter how old you are, how smart you are, or what color you skin is. Instead, you find yourself within a group where every individual knows how you feel.

Empathy is extraordinarily powerful. People love it when they feel they are being understood and that their thoughts and feelings are legitimate and valued. We want people to know and respect how we feel.

Unfortunately, most companies never get past the first step when it comes to empathy. Companies don't care at all how you feel. They care only about what you do. They want you to buy stuff from them. They will certainly identify what they think you and people like you are feeling. But they are motivated not by genuine concern for you. They simply want to find a new angle that will help them craft more effective marketing messages.

So now we come full circle again and find another reason why finding stuff out from the expert next door is so attractive to so many people.

Individuals are almost always more empathetic than companies or other large organizations. When did you last feel empathy pouring out from a government website?

But when you, as an individual, write a website you can write in a way that is extremely empathetic. Like the nurse, you need to combine your empathy with a solid body of knowledge and useful information. Succeed in that and you will create a site that people naturally feel drawn to. They will feel a kinship with who you are and what you say. Your right-brain approach will make them feel good, and offer a much needed respite from the left-brain sites of large organizations.

Thousands of people are using this approach to create profitable websites right now.

Think of a topic, just about any topic. Chances are that someone out there has built a website and is writing a very useful, empathetic body of information to share with his or her readers.

These sites may not receive millions of visitors, but many are attracting tens of thousands of readers a month.

My CoffeeDetective.com site falls in the middle ground. It gets more visitors than many sites, but far fewer than some others. How many? At the time of writing it gets about 40,000 unique visits a month. There are successful local newspapers and magazines out there with fewer readers than that. And, of course, I don't have their overheads to worry about. Also I know people working on their sites from home who get ten times that amount of traffic.

What are people writing about? Here are a few examples.

Adventure vacations. Divorce. Learning a language. Making wooden toys. Juggling. Martial arts. Training parrots. Organic recipes. Hiking. Home decoration. Baking cakes. Restoring antiques. Hair care. How to draw. How to write. Guitar lessons. Making gift baskets. Song writing. Kid's crafts. Herbal medicine. Tax advice. Home office design. Auto repair. Travel guides. Photography tips. Mountain bike riding. Children's parties. Flower arrangements. Online game tips.

Multiply that list by a thousand and you'll just be scratching the surface of topics you can address through your own website. Think of some areas in which you already have some knowledge and interest. Then decide to share that knowledge with other people.

In doing so you will be taking on the mantle of the expert next door. This doesn't mean you need any formal qualifications in that area. You simply have to know more than most of your neighbors, real and virtual.

Information from the expert next door is becoming more and more attractive as an alternative to the authorized, left-brain packaged and approved information we are fed by big media.

For all the reasons outlined in this chapter, you are ideally placed to grow an audience of engaged and enthusiastic readers.

CHAPTER FOUR

SAY THANK YOU TO GOOGLE FOR MAKING ALL THIS POSSIBLE

Google certainly wasn't the first search engine, nor is it the only one. But it is, by far, the biggest. So rather than provide a list of different search engines in each paragraph I write, I'll simply refer to Google. The principles I am going to discuss apply equally to all the major players.

First, let's step back and take a broad view of what the existence of search engines actually means to us.

Go back twenty years and imagine that you wanted to start a print publication about building and installing garden bridges. People have these as decorative accents, sometimes as a span over an actual stream or pond, or spanning a faux stream made of pebbles and rocks. It's a pretty narrow topic.

Twenty years ago, before you decided to publish, you would have figured out the content and structure of what you could write, including major subject areas and numerous, more detailed sub-topics. You could have used photos, provided blueprints for the do-it-yourself crowd, written about ponds, about plants, and so on.

Once you had figured out what to say, you would have had to ask yourself one or both of the following questions.

1. How can I reach an audience of people who will be interested in learning about garden bridges?

2. How can I sell and distribute my publication?

In the world of old media, these are tough questions.

A mainstream book publisher isn't going to be interested, because your topic is way too narrow. They won't feel confident that they can reach enough people, sell enough copies of your book and actually make some money.

So then you approach some gardening magazines, and they tell you that while they might be interested in a single 750-word article on the topic, that is about as far as they will go.

Discouraged, you decide to publish the information yourself, in the form of a printed Garden Bridge newsletter. You know there are thousands of people who would be interested. But how on earth are you going to find these people, let them know what you are offering and then persuade them to subscribe? Remember, this is twenty years ago, before the days of the Web. Maybe you could buy some classified ads in garden-related magazines? You could, but it would cost a bit and you would have to advertise in many different places repeatedly to reach the people you are looking for.

Before the Web many people and companies did succeed with printed newsletters, but they were almost all focused on topics which have mass appeal—like healthy living, losing weight and making money.

Finally, you shelve the idea and put all your notes into a box in the basement.

Before the days of the Web it was very, very hard for an individual with a narrow area of passion and expertise to become a publisher.

But now you can. For just a few dollars you can buy a domain name—GardenBridgeDesigns.com, for example—and start publishing some useful and interesting content.

Will your new website be found? Not on day one it won't. And there are things you will need to do to ensure that Google both finds your site and likes it enough to list you on the first page of results when someone searches for the term "garden bridge designs."

But at least you'll be there. You'll be able to tell your friends about it, mention it on your Facebook page, and in forums, and so on. (We'll talk more about ways to get traffic to your new website later.)

We have now crossed the first hurdle. While traditional publishers may not be willing to publish your work, the Web has enabled you to do it yourself. The Web enables anyone to become a publisher, and Google provides the opportunity for your site to be found by anyone and everyone who is interested in your topic.

This first part of the equation is enabled by the existence and popularity of the Web itself.

The second part comes as a direct result of the existence of the search engines, particularly Google.

Why Google changes everything.

In common with other online tools and services, it is all too easy to take the search engines for granted. But they are massive game-changers.

What Google does is take the control of content selection out of the hands of big media and hands it over both to online publishers and, more importantly, to the billion people who use the Web.

As I mentioned earlier, it used to be that the content we found in traditional media was chosen by big media themselves. They decided what we should see, hear, and read. And they certainly wouldn't devote an hour of prime-time TV to building garden bridges.

Online, it is ultimately the user who is in control...the reader, listener, and viewer. If I want to learn about garden bridges I can simply type those words into a search engine and see what comes up. Before I try, I won't know whether I'll get any quality results. But at least I can make up my own mind about what I want to learn about, and I can give it a shot. Before the arrival of the Web and search engines, I didn't even have that choice. I had no way of scouring the globe and finding possible results within a fraction of a second.

Now pause a minute and think of the implications when not one, but one billion people think and act in the same way. Instead of leafing through numerous magazines in search of a particular answer they are looking for, they instead turn to Google.

Aggregate all that activity and you will see how the act of using search engines turns publishing on its head. Instead of publishers deciding what people should be reading, the public decides on what they want for themselves. They vote by typing in search terms. Billions of times a day. Look at what people search for and you'll find out what they really want to know.

The public, the consumers of information, never really had a means to make their voices and preferences heard before now. The search engines give them that voice. And now everyone online knows that they don't have to wait on a newspaper, magazine, or book publisher to finally deliver the information they really want. Instead, they can go to Google and find that information instantly.

The lesson for publishers both large and small is this: Stop guessing at what people want, or trying to *make* people want what you currently deliver, just listen carefully to what they are asking for. Google can help us listen.

A big media editor may tell you that barely anyone is interested in garden bridges. An analysis of search data at Google may tell you that over 40,000 people worldwide made searches related to garden bridges last month alone.

Now look at this another way. If you had published that paper newsletter you would have had to struggle to let those 40,000 people know about it. Actually, it would have been an impossible task. Some of those people would be in North America, some in Europe, some in Asia, and so on. You could never have got in front of everyone with your message.

But when you make friends with Google, the geometry is reversed. You no longer have to try reaching those people. You wait for Google to send them to you. You simply write and create your website in a way that Google likes. Your job as a publisher is no longer about marketing and distribution, it is about focusing on creating high quality content. It's no longer about pushing, it's about attracting. Do that, and Google will do the rest for you.

And yes, this means you can go head-to-head with major gardening publications, both offline and online and win. How so? Because those big publications have to focus on hundreds of different aspects of gardening and garden design. But your site will focus much more narrowly, just on garden bridges.

So when someone searches for "garden bridge designs," Google will quite rightly determine that your site is probably the better match. There are other factors involved in how high up Google places your site in its listings, but writing great content on a narrow topic gives you a definite advantage.

Now for the catch.

It's wonderful to know that Google is out there, sending visitors to your websites. It actually feels too good to be true. In the world of old media you had to pay through the nose on advertising to get people to come to your store or find out about your products and services. And now the search engines find your site, send you traffic—and they don't charge you a penny.

Naturally, there is a catch. Whatever the topic you choose, hundreds or thousands of people will already have written web pages devoted to that topic. In other words, you will be competing for Google's attention.

As an example, my site CoffeeDetective.com is all about coffee. But if you type the word *coffee* into Google and start looking for my site, you'll have to go all the way to the 21st page of results until you find it. In other words, over 200 other sites come ahead of mine.

How many people are going to scroll through 21 pages and then decide to learn about coffee from my site? None. Zero. Almost everyone will choose one of the websites that are on page one.

So how on earth do I get any traffic from Google?

I find niche topics. I find aspects of making coffee that are not dealt with in detail on those other 200 or so websites. Now go back to Google and type in the term *organic coffee pods*. At the time of writing, my page on this topic is listed number one on Google. Coffee pods are like plump tea bags and are used in single serve coffee makers. And some people who use these brewers and buy coffee pods want to find out about the availability of organic coffee pods. So they type that phrase into Google and plenty of them click on the first listing, which is mine.

You might be saying to yourself, "But compared to the number of people who search for *coffee*, the number of people searching for *organic coffee pods* must be tiny."

Yes and no.

Yes, plenty of people will search for the word *coffee*. But that's why I have over 700 pages on my website, with most of them focused on narrow topics of interest, like organic coffee pods. Instead of going head-to-head on the primary topics, I choose instead to write on topics about which there is a narrower interest, but far fewer websites competing for attention.

Also, people don't search for the single word *coffee* as often as you might think. Over recent years there has been a trend towards people using longer, more specific terms when they do a search.

To get away from coffee for a moment, imagine that you are thinking of vacationing in Mexico and like the idea of lying on the beach. You are not going to go to Google and type in the single word *mexico* or *vacations*. If you did, you know you would find a huge list of irrelevant results. Instead you type in *beach vacation in mexico* or something like that.

Searchers are becoming more sophisticated in their use of search engines, and they know that a broad, single-word term is unlikely to deliver useful, relevant results.

In other words, as the writer of CoffeeDetective.com, I'm really not interested in competing for the word *coffee* in the search engines. I would rather be number one for a more specific term like *is coffee fattening?* And if I write hundreds of pages, many of them giving me Google search results within the first page, I'll probably get more traffic than those guys who get on page one for the term *coffee*.

The two things you need to know about how Google works.

If you want to do well on Google, and you do, because the search traffic they send you will cost you nothing but the time you spend writing your pages, then you need to understand what Google does, and what it is looking for.

What I am going to describe is a simplification of a massively complex process, driven by algorithms that would make Einstein's head spin. But behind that complexity lies a couple of very simple principles.

The first thing to get right...

Make it easy for Google to figure out what your website pages are about.

Google sends out small software bots which follow links from site to site, across the Web. When it finds a new page, it indexes it. But to make sense of a page, a simple piece of software has to determine what the page is *about*. It's not a human looking at your page, it's a piece of software. It can't look at your graphics, nor can it reach an intuitive understanding of what you are talking about on a particular page. It can only read the text on the page, and from that it has to figure out the subject of the page.

So when someone does that search for *beach vacation in mexico*, Google will look through its database and try to find the pages that are the best match for that phrase.

This has serious implications for us as writers. It means that when we write that page, we need to make it abundantly clear what the page is about.

One of the best ways to do that is to confine each page to a single topic.

That piece of advice alone can transform the performance of your website. Take that long page about beaches in South America and think about how it could be broken up into several pages, each of them focused on a particular area in South America.

If someone types in that search *beach vacation in mexico* and your page covers beaches in Mexico, Brazil, and a few other countries, Google will struggle to figure out what your page is really about. You might actually have the best content about Mexican beaches, but Google won't know that, because you're also talking about Brazil.

Does this mean you have to write each page just to appeal to a small piece of software? Absolutely not. You write it for your reader. When I wrote my page about whether coffee is fattening, I confined the page precisely to that topic. I did that as a service to my readers, because someone looking for information about whether coffee is fattening is looking for information about that specific topic, not about whether a blade coffee grinder is as good as a burr coffee grinder. I don't mix topics on a single page. That makes it easier for my readers to find exactly what they want, and easier for Google to identify the topic of each page.

How come Google's software works like this? Because Google puts the reader first. Google tries to emulate the priorities of a reader, because the reputation of its service depends on pleasing its human users.

Put simply, if you write pages designed to help your readers, you will be pleasing Google at the same time.

Here is the second thing to get right...

Not only should you be writing great content for your readers, you also want to impress the heck out of your peers. In other words, you want a lot of quality, established websites linking back to yours.

Why is this? Because without looking at your inbound links, Google has no way to know whether or not your page is any good. Their bot wanders around and does a good job of identifying the topic of each of your web pages, but the bot is just code, and it can't make a value judgement on the quality of those pages.

How can Google determine the quality of a page or, indeed, of your entire site? It takes a look at who else out there is linking to you.

This process is borrowed from the academic world, where papers are judged, in part, by the quantity and quality of peer reviews. Peer reviews and the standing of the people who write the reviews, give others a good insight as to the quality of your work. If very smart and established people write a glowing review of your work, that gives it the academic equivalent of two thumbs up.

Google applies the same principle to websites. If Starbucks added a link to my CoffeeDetective.com website (never going to happen), Google would find that link from Starbucks to my site and would draw some conclusions. Basically, it would think, in so far as software can think, "Wow, if a site as established and as popular as Starbucks is linking to CoffeeDetective.com on its home page, then this other site *must* be good."

We'll talk more about linking strategies later on. But you need to be aware of this. Your site has to be useful and interesting enough to encourage people to link to it. And, given the volume of competition out there, your site had better be a little different in some way. You need to stand out and attract attention, and you need to leverage that attention by having plenty of people linking to your site.

Being friends with Google isn't so hard.

If you want to be friends with Google—and get a flood of free search engine traffic coming to your site—job one is to be friends with your readers.

If you write a great site that is put together with a view to really and truly helping people who share an interest in your topic, then you'll be 90% of the way to pleasing Google.

As for the last 10%, Google actually goes to great lengths to let people know the best way to please them. They have published a set of guidelines for webmasters, and also offer a range of webmaster tools to help you get things right. They are totally upfront about what they are looking for in a good site and are generous in providing you with the tools to make it happen.

CHAPTER FIVE

WHEN LOOKING FOR A TOPIC FOR YOUR WEBSITE, FIND THE GAP

By now you should be getting a good idea of the big picture.

The Web has transformed the world of publishing. A billion Web users are now also writers and publishers. We no longer need the permission of editors. Nor do we have to pay for the printing and distribution of our work. Best of all, Google will send us visitors, at no charge.

But how do you choose a topic for your website? How can you decide on a subject that not only interests you, but will also stand a chance of being found when people conduct searches on the major search engines like Google? How do you get your website listed on the first page of results? How do you get noticed?

This is important, because the new path to riches model is based on receiving a ton of free traffic from the search engines. Almost all the people who visit CoffeeDetective.com arrive via the search engines. And most of them arrive after finding one of my site's pages listed on Google.

The foundation of this model is based on *finding the gap*.

By a gap I mean that you need to find a slice of a topic about which people are interested, but for which there is not an overwhelming supply of quality information available online already.

For instance, I wouldn't try writing a website on the topic of auto insurance. There is already a massive supply of information online, and some big players spend a lot on advertising to attract traffic. As someone working from home, it makes no sense to deliberately set out to compete against such strong competitors.

Besides which, the topic of auto insurance lends itself very well to a company, but not so well to the "expert next door." I would ask my neighbor for advice about growing roses, but probably not about the finer points of auto insurance. There are some topics about which we understandably want to defer to a professional. For the same reason, I wouldn't write a website about dental care, unless I was a dentist.

Which topics work best for a money-making website? There are no hard and fast rules, but a simple rule of thumb is to look first at topics which relate to what people do in their spare time.

Think about what people do when they get home from work.

What do people like to do after they leave work for the day, or at the weekends? These topics are a great place to start looking, for a few reasons. First, it takes you out of the realm of competing with professionals, like auto insurance companies and dentists. Second, it takes people into areas of personal interest and passion.

Except for the fortunate few, most people are not totally passionate about their jobs. They get much more excited about what they do when they get home, whether that be bird watching, cooking, child raising, cycling, bar hopping, driving, playing video games, sailing, learning to play guitar, reading, watching movies, horse riding, furniture restoration, amateur drama, sewing, pet care, traveling, working out, and so on.

The fact that people are passionate about these hobbies and interests gives you, as a writer, an edge. It means these people are genuinely interested in knowing more. This is the stuff they love to do. And they love to learn.

What are your own interests? What do you do when you get home or at the weekend? As I have mentioned before, you don't need to be a qualified expert in that area. You just need to be interested in it, and to know more than most other people. And knowing more about a subject than most other people isn't so hard.

When you write a website about a hobby or personal area of interest, you will still be competing with companies who are in the same space. For instance, my coffee site competes for attention with Starbucks. But that's okay. Because Starbucks and I have sites with quite different purposes. Theirs is focused on promoting Starbucks, and mine is focused on helping people make better gourmet coffee at home. Whatever the topic, there will always be some overlap with what large companies are doing. Don't worry about that. Your site will be very different than theirs.

Choose a topic that focuses on something people like to do in their spare time, and you'll have put yourself in the perfect position to become the expert next door. When it comes to hobbies, people love to learn from each other. Sure, they might buy some books on their topic of interest, but they will also connect with others who are not qualified experts but do share their passion.

Take cooking, for example. Yes, there are books you can buy, TV shows you can watch and DVD sets you can purchase. But people who like to cook have also created a vibrant community among themselves online. Through websites, blogs, and social media platforms, people passionate about cooking are constantly sharing recipes, tips and tricks.

Take a quick look at WhatToCookWhen.com. It's a blog written by Rebecca Matter. She's not a professional chef. But she loves to cook and is passionate about sharing what she knows. She writes blog posts, adds photos, and also creates short how-to videos. And yes, she gets a ton of visitors who love what she does. What is the gap she has found? It ties to the word *when* in her domain name. The blog isn't just about cooking, it's about what to cook when...when you have friends over, when the boss comes for dinner, when you are short of time, when you want to BBQ. That's her niche, that's her gap.

Cooking is a perfect example of where the expert next door can compete with the professionals. When we are learning about a hobby or interest we don't want to learn only from professionals, we also want to connect with others who share the same passion. That's why there are cycling clubs, sewing circles, drama groups. We want to share and to be included.

These are the areas to watch for. When you write about a hobby or interest, you immediately put yourself in an area that is outside of the influence of big business. We don't want big business to be part of our club or group. They don't belong. We may turn to them for products and services, but not for conversation and networking.

Now ask yourself, what do you know?

What do you already know about? What are your own hobbies? Also, allow yourself the possibility of a cross-over between your work and your interest.

For instance, I know someone who is a professional videographer. He shoots and edits videos for a living. In that world he is a professional.

But he also likes to share what he knows with the millions of people who are making their own videos for sites like YouTube. He simply takes his professional knowledge and then presents it in a way that is useful for regular people who want to make short videos with their home computers. For this latter audience he is the expert next door, not the industry professional. He writes in a way that works for non-professionals.

Maybe your own work has given you an expertise that is also of interest to non-professionals.

In my own case, I have no background in the coffee industry. But a few years ago I had a contract to do some writing for an online coffee company. It was a professional relationship. The contract lasted for about six months, during which time I learned a great deal about coffee and coffee making. And I found that I had quite an interest in the topic, on a personal level.

So I leveraged what I had learned during those six months and started writing my coffee site. Did I know enough even to call myself an "expert next door" in the early days? Probably not. But I started anyway. And the more I wrote, and the more I listened to what my readers were asking, the more I learned. And now, yes I am an expert next door. Now I know more about the topic than most non-professionals, and am in a very good position to help other people who are starting out on their love affair with quality coffee.

What do you know about? What interests you? What can you imagine yourself writing about? Remember, to create a large and successful site that can make you money, you are going to have to write plenty of pages. You don't have to write them all in the first month, but after a year or so you should have over a hundred pages. I hesitate to say that, because some people might feel intimidated by that kind of number. If I had thought about it myself I might not have started my coffee site. How many pages can you write about coffee? It turns out that there appears to be no limit. People will always have new questions, companies will always launch new coffees, coffee makers, and coffee grinders.

Now find the gap within your subject area.

Rebecca Matter found a gap in her cooking topic by adding the word "when" to her domain name. She noticed that while there were a lot of blogs and websites about cooking, there wasn't much about cooking for specific events or occasions.

There are several ways to look for a gap and here are some of them.

1. <u>Find a gap in the level of audience expertise being addressed.</u>

What's my gap with the CoffeeDetective.com site? Good question. On the face of it, it looks like I was mad to try competing with hundreds of coffee companies, coffee roasters, and coffee shops. How would my site stand out? How could I compete for attention on Google? I found my gap by not trying to appeal to every coffee lover. My site specifically targets beginners.

When looking at coffee sites I found that most of them were talking to people who already knew quite a bit about coffee. Nearly every site and blog and forum I went to were addressing the "coffee geeks." These are the people who freak out if you brew your coffee with water that is two degrees too hot. What I didn't find was a body of information for people who were just starting out. It turns out there are a huge number of people who haven't made gourmet coffee at home before, and don't know simple things like how much coffee to add to their brewer when making six cups of coffee. I had found my gap...the beginners.

You can address any topic in this way. If you want to write a site about learning to play the guitar, you can segment your potential audience into beginners, intermediate, and experts. Which level of expertise best suits your own level of knowledge? Which area is not yet being very well served by existing websites?

Go to Google yourself and enter a phrase or word that best describes your topic. Now look through the sites that are listed on the first two pages of results. Vary the key phrase a little and explore some other sites in the same way. Look at those websites through a lens which segments between beginner, intermediate, and expert. You may find that one of those levels of expertise is not being very well addressed.

2. Look for a gap in quality.

When you do a search for your topic on Google, first impressions can be scary. You may find that Google has found hundreds of thousands or even millions of pages that match your search query.

Before you panic, look through the sites on those first two pages of results and ask yourself whether or not the information they provide is of high quality. Is the information truly useful? Are the sites attractive and well organized? Will readers find it easy to find what they are looking for? Are the information needs of their readers taken good care of?

Recently I did a search for the term *manual watch repair.* There were plenty of results, but there were very, very few quality results. That may not be a topic for which there is a big demand these days. It's probably not a good topic for me to pursue if I want to create another money-making website. However, it does demonstrate that while Google might show a lot of results for a search, it doesn't mean that those results automatically indicate a body of quality, useful information.

Take a look at your topic from a few different angles and see if you can find a gap in the amount of quality information currently available.

3. <u>Look for a gap with subject niches.</u>

Most topics can be sub-divided into numerous different niche topics. As an example, again in the realm of coffee, I have a second website called OneCupCoffeeReviews.com. It focuses on just one vertical segment of coffee as a whole. It's about single-serve coffee making. Single serve coffee makers use sealed cups, pods or discs, each filled with enough ground coffee for one cup of coffee. These are a convenient, if slightly more expensive way, to make your morning coffee.

What is the benefit of picking a niche like this? First, it takes you out of the big crowd that surrounds any primary topic. I'm no longer competing for attention when people search for information on coffee. I'm competing only with a far smaller group of websites which talk specifically about single-serve coffee.

By picking a niche within a primary topic you are also narrowing the audience you have to appeal to. If you write a website about tea, then you are trying to write to a very broad audience, some who like a regular tea, others who love green tea, and others who can tell the difference between teas grown in adjoining regions in India. It's tough to write well to a crowd as broad as that. Everything you write will appeal to one segment of your audience, but will fail to engage the majority. By choosing one niche, like green tea, you can write pages which appeal to everyone who comes to the site.

Here are a few more examples of how you can pick a niche from within a primary topic.

Instead of writing about dog food, write about organic dog food.

Instead of writing about bicycles, write about mountain bikes.

Instead of writing about desserts, write about desserts from the Middle East.

Instead of writing about home decoration, write about home decoration projects which can be completed in a weekend.

Instead of writing about high tech gadgets, write about high tech gadgets for the disabled.

Instead of writing reviews of TV shows, write reviews of shows that can be streamed via the Internet.

Whatever your broad interest, there are many different ways to slice and dice it. List some niche options, and then do some research through Google to find out which niches attract a large number of searches, but are served by relatively few quality websites.

4. <u>Find a gap by watching regional and global movements in fads and products.</u>

This may sound a little fancy, but it needn't be. Several months ago, I did a search on Google for the single word, "headphones." The first page of search results showed that three out of the ten sites listed were from the UK, with co.uk domains. Another site was from Australia with a com.au domain. This caught my attention because I was searching from a computer in Montreal, Canada. Given a choice, Google likes to deliver search results from domains which are based at least within the same continent. The fact that forty percent of the first page results were not based in North America told me that Google was having trouble finding quality results.

Something else. Three of the other results were from intermediaries like Amazon and BestBuy. Sure, these sites sell headphones, but they aren't a great source of in-depth information on the topic. At the time (and I see the mix of search results has now changed), there were only two out of ten sites on the first page of search results that offered readers helpful, detailed information about headphones.

To me, that looked like a pretty nice gap. It seemed that in the UK and in Australia people were already interested in trading up from the horrible earbuds that came with their MP3 players. And it struck me that it was only a matter of time before iPod owners in North America decided they wanted to do the same. I didn't have the time to make much of that opportunity, but it was interesting to identify the gap.

Here's another example. In North America we sometimes feel that all the best technological advances come from here and then spread out across the world. Not so. It often happens the other way around. Going back to the topic of single serve brewers, they became popular in Europe before catching the attention of consumers over here. Jay Brewer anticipated the trend and created a blog called SingleServeCoffee.com. He saw a possible trend and jumped in ahead of the competition. As a result, he has done very, very well. And all he does is write about single serve coffee makers. And yes, single serve coffee makers did jump the pond and are now very popular over here.

All that said, and hats off to Jay Brewer, you don't have to be the first to identify a new trend or niche. It is very, very tough to find any kind of niche that has no competition. At least, it is hard to find a niche with no competition for which there is significant demand. But that's okay. You don't have to be the first, or the only one in your niche. You just have to get away from the big crowd of competitors which fight for attention in the primary topic area. Being the tenth or twentieth or fiftieth website in a niche is okay. You just have to work hard to make your site different, more informative, and more useful. Remember, Google will always look kindly on a site that is packed with useful, relevant, and quality information.

5. <u>Find a gap by age groups, life events, or segments within the population.</u>

It would be tough to get much traffic to your site if you wrote it just about yoga. There are a ton of quality sites about that subject already.

But how about yoga for children? Yoga for teens? Yoga for the elderly?

Or look at life events. Yoga for pregnant women. Yoga for the retired.

Maybe you would like to write about amateur theater. You can focus on age groups, but also by specific segments within the population. How about amateur theater for troubled teens? Amateur theater for people in wheelchairs?

Write about baseball for seniors, cooking for busy couples, learning English for recent immigrants.

All I am doing here is suggesting a range of different lenses through which to search for niche areas within otherwise broad topics.

6. Segment by passion, cause, or belief.

Don't write about fruits and vegetables, write about Fair Trade fruits and vegetables. By the way, this niche is also a geographical or trending niche. Interest in Fair Trade foods has a much deeper penetration in England than it does in North America right now. Many English supermarkets have entire aisles devoted to Fair Trade produce. Will the trend grow in the US and Canada? If you believe it will, now might be a good time to start writing about it.

Many people believe in buying organic foods. Others are passionate about going green with their cars. How about vegetarian food? Kosher desserts? Wind power? Food that isn't genetically modified? Using grey water in the garden? Using non-toxic cleaning products? Recycling?

Is there a subject about which you are passionate? Something that gets you excited or makes you angry? Something you really believe in?

If so, if you are true believer in your area of interest, pay close attention to that. The great thing about true believers is that they are passionate about what they do, they want to spread the word and they want others to share their passions and beliefs. I'm not talking about religion here, I'm talking more about social causes that touch people's emotions.

As an example, there is a question-and-answer thread at CoffeeDetective.com that started with someone asking about whether there was a coffee maker that had no plastic parts. The writer was concerned that the hot water would leach chemicals like BPA out of the plastic. I answered the question as best I could and was then amazed by the number of people adding comments to the thread. It seems a lot of people are concerned about BPA and other chemicals used in plastics which come into contact with our food and drinks.

There is a niche there, not just about coffee makers, but about every gadget and implement we have in our kitchens. And it's an interesting niche because it touches on a topic that people get very passionate and heated about. Am I going to pursue that niche? No, I'm not. It's not that I don't believe there are harmful chemicals used in food packaging and kitchen implements. I'm quite sure there are. And I do care about that. But I don't feel passionate about it. It's just not for me. There are only so many causes we can truly feel passionate about, and for me that isn't one of them. If I did create a website on that topic, I would be doing so simply because I figured I could make a few dollars from my readers. And it wouldn't take them long to find me out. The coffee site works for me because, although there is no cause there, I am genuinely interested in helping people enjoy better coffee.

Remember that. Your website will always be better if your interest is genuine.

Also, remember that you don't need to reach a huge audience in order to make some money. You're not big media. You just need to reach a small but passionate audience that loves the information you provide. As individuals, as experts next door, this is our advantage.

We can make a very nice second or even first income by appealing to a relatively narrow segment of the population.

7. Explore the long tail.

You will always do better if your pages are aimed at a particular slice of a topic that is popular among searchers, but for which there is little quality information provided elsewhere. The more pages you create which are focused on these narrow slices of information, the higher your pages will appear in the relevant search results. For example, your website will likely appear higher in the search results if you write a page about *rust-resistant roses* than one about *roses*.

This multitude of slices is often referred to as the long tail. The head is the word *rose*, and you will face a ton of heavy competition from established gardening sites for that one word. The tail is comprised of all the multi-word terms about roses for which there is much less completion. As an example, the term *growing roses in cold climates* is a long tail phrase. It is very specific and if you write a page just on that topic you will have a good chance of beating other, more established sites which don't have a separate page focused on that search phrase.

Focusing on the long tail is key to success in the new path to riches model. It is part and parcel of finding the gap. Big sites do very well for words and phrases that are close to the "head" of any given topic. But they don't do so well in the tail.

For the term *coffee*, Starbucks ranks number one in the Google search results. For the long tail term *is coffee fattening?* CoffeeDetective.com is number one. It is the very existence of the long tail online that makes it possible for small entrepreneurs like you and me to make money with our websites.

To get a broader sense of how the Web has changed things, consider your local music store. It is of a fixed and limited size. There is only so much shelf space. So the owner stocks those shelves with best sellers. It's not that people don't want to buy less popular music, it's just that the owner doesn't have the physical space to offer everything.

It's the same with books. Amazon has millions of books listed on its site. That's a whole lot more titles than you can fit in even the largest bricks and mortar store. Also, consider iTunes and the number of songs it has for sale. Yes, both Amazon and iTunes stock and sell the bestsellers. But they generate more total sales from the long tail. Neither is confined within the fixed dimensions of a physical store, and the addition of a lot more titles costs them very little.

Whatever the topic, people are not just interested in bestsellers, or in just the primary topic descriptions, like *coffee*, *roses* and *travel*. Millions of people are looking for specific, detailed information that resides not at the head, but somewhere in the long tail.

In the physical world you can readily find books on roses, but you are unlikely to find books on long tail segments of the topic, like *organic compost for roses*.

This where your website comes in. It will give your readers the information they can't easily find in books, magazines, or on major websites.

Most of your pages should be focused very clearly on long tail search terms, with just one term per page. If you are writing a page about *organic compost for roses*, confine the page to that topic only. Use that exact term in the page title. Use it in the page's description field. Use it in the page's headline.

When you repeat the phrase in these high-visibility places on your page, you are letting your readers know exactly what the page is about. You are also letting Google know what the page is about, without any uncertainty or confusion.

If you can find long tail terms for which there is a high number of searches, but with relatively few pages of quality content competing for attention, you'll be golden.

Find the gap that maximizes the income potential of your website.

This is a tricky area.

When they start out researching and writing a website, too many people have their eyes firmly fixed on the money they can make. It's all about maximizing keyword research, maximizing traffic, maximizing conversion rates, and making a ton of cash.

Unfortunately, this approach rarely works. Why not? Because your visitors quickly figure out that your primary purpose is not to help and inform them, but to make money from them. And that's not a very nice feeling.

The best, and most successful approach is to keep your eyes not on the money but on the quality and value of the pages you write. Over-deliver on quality. Make your site the most helpful in its class.

That said, you need to keep half an eye on the income potential of your site. If you only focus on the quality of the content, you could end up with a wonderful website and an income of $10 a month. That's not much of a return on a great deal of work.

The secret here is to maintain the right balance. Don't focus only on the quality of content. And definitely don't focus only on making money. Balance both needs at the same time.

For instance I might write a fantastic, useful, and passionate website about the growth of bacteria in Arctic ice. It could be the most informative site of its kind. But, how would I make money from that site?

Finding the right gap is also about timing.

A quality information website that also makes good money often positions itself just before the moment when someone wants to buy something.

When I write a page on my coffee site comparing three different coffee makers, people will come there because they are about to buy a new coffee maker and want to know which one to choose. In other words, they have found my page immediately before the moment of finally choosing a brewer and making the purchase. So if that page includes an affiliate link to a merchant who sells those brewers, then I stand a reasonable chance that some of my readers will click on that link and make a purchase from the merchant site. When that happens, I make a commission.

However, if I write a page about the countries where coffee comes from, my readers are unlikely to be in "buying mode." They are probably just satisfying a moment of curiosity. They just want to learn something. I'm unlikely to make any money from visitors to that page, but if I write it well enough they might bookmark or remember my site and come back at another time when they are thinking about buying something.

Coffee is not a bad subject for a site because people do buy coffee makers, and they also buy coffee on an ongoing basis. But as always, I think in terms of balance. I don't write pages only for people who are about to buy. I also write pages for people who simply want to learn. Doing so gives my site more credibility. It also builds trust and respect. If someone habitually comes to my site just to learn about various aspects of coffee, maybe they'll trust me to give them some good advice on the day they want to buy a new brewer. By building a reputation as an authority on coffee, and as a trustworthy source of information, I ultimately increase the number of visitors who want sound advice during the moments before they actually make a purchase.

As you plan, research, and develop your topic ideas, think about this. When you consider your audience, what purchases might they make after reading pages on your site? Are you creating a site that is a good place to visit just before someone goes to a merchant site and makes a purchase?

This is an important consideration when you build a site with the specific purpose of generating income.

Be the trustworthy expert next door. And choose a topic that enables you to deliver sound, honest advice in the moments just before your readers are ready to buy something. By positioning your site in this way you will be maximizing the opportunity to make income through merchant affiliate links.

While going through this process, also consider the cost of the items or services your readers are about to buy. If the cost per unit is high, your commissions are also likely to be high. If the cost is low, that's not so good.

I experience both ends of the spectrum on my coffee site. When someone comes to my site, follows one of my affiliate links and buys one pound of coffee, I might earn $1.95. At that rate I'll need a huge number of visitors in order to make a reasonable income from my site. But when someone buys a coffee maker or an espresso machine, I might make $20 or $40 in commissions. That's a big jump and it's the reason why most of the income from my coffee sites comes to me through the sale of coffee equipment, and not through the sale of coffee itself.

Yes, there are plenty of lenses to look through when finding a gap.

This entire chapter has been about finding the right gap for your new website. And yes, there are numerous different ways to look at a gap. Is it a niche that has a large enough audience? Is there room for a different or better website in that niche? Does it interest you? Are there a sufficient number of relevant keywords or phrases to attract plenty of search engine traffic? Are you reaching people at a time when they are ready to buy? What is the cost of what they might buy?

You need to look at your site topic through all of these lenses and make a note of what you see. It is unlikely you will find a topic that is an absolute star in every respect. But you do need to find some strength in each area.

You don't have to get it all right on day one.

If you think your site has at least some potential, based on the criteria above, go for it. What will happen is that you will write the first twenty of so pages, and then, as people come to your site, you will start learning.

Now it's time for me to make a confession. Earlier in this chapter I wrote that I deliberately started writing my site CoffeeDetective.com with the clear intention of focusing on beginners. That's not quite true. When I started out, I didn't have a fixed idea of the exact direction I was moving in, although I did want to focus on the basics of coffee making. It was only after I started listening to my readers that I realized that my audience really were beginners. I fine-tuned my focus and wrote more and more for beginners. I listened carefully and gave my readers more of what they wanted.

Also, I didn't find any really good affiliate partnerships within the first few months. Getting that right came later as well.

The point is, you do all you can before you choose your topic and start writing your site. But you don't have to get everything right on day one. It probably isn't even possible. Just start as best you can and then keep learning as you go along. For as long as you are listening, you'll always find new ways to add value to your site and please your visitors.

That's the great thing about websites...they are never finished. It's not like a book where you have to write a final draft and can't change a thing once the book is printed. With a website you can always add new material, edit existing pages, add graphics and videos, change the design...and so on.

This means you can create something today and then keep improving it for months and years to come. It's a work in progress.

Big media delivers the information *they* want to share. You deliver the information *your readers are actually looking for.*

Here is another, large gap.

Think back to the earlier chapters of this book. Big media publishers have a plan. They sit down and decide on what their readers, listeners, and viewers are going to learn and experience.

Our approach, which is also our advantage, is very different. We don't decide on what our readers *should* learn from us. We publish the information they *want* to learn about.

That is a profound difference, and it is one that is possible only because of all the tools and resources that come with the Web.

It is possible now to find out how many other sites publish information on a particular topic or niche. It is also possible to find out exactly what people are looking for and even the exact phrases they use in their searches.

This enables us to create website content that is precisely in tune with what people actually want.

Big media could do the same, using the same kinds of tools, but they don't. They have other agendas to follow. They have services and products to sell. Their marketing and PR teams tell them what "messaging" to use. Their legal teams tell them which words they can and can't use.

Big media is driven by considerations that are internal.

Small media, that's you and me, are driven by recognition of what our audience actually wants and needs. Our considerations are external.

This is a gap we can fill. And this is why many one-person websites often get higher listings than large corporate sites for the identical search phrase. A one-person site can write a page focused precisely on the term *Costa Rica beaches*. A large company site will add a bunch of other content to that page, maybe promoting a last minute deal to Cancun in Mexico. They add the deal because they want to make money. But when Google looks at their page, their software isn't quite sure whether the page is about Costa Rica beaches or Cancun. Quite correctly, Google concludes that yours is the more relevant page and may list you higher in the search results.

Creating websites that are driven in response to what our audience actually wants helps us create content that is relevant, engaging, useful, and appreciated.

We are the anti-big-media and our readers love us for it.

CHAPTER SIX

HOW TO MAKE YOUR READERS LIKE YOU

Several years ago I used to do quite a bit of public speaking at Internet marketing conferences. The first time I did it was pretty scary. I had never spoken to a group of more than maybe ten people in a business setting. Suddenly I was on a platform in front of about seven hundred people. I went through my presentation and I did okay. Not good, but okay.

At the end of the day I sat down with the organizers and went through the feedback from the audience. My presentation was right there in the middle. Not good, not bad, but okay.

I hated that. I hate being just okay. Anyway, I asked if they would be bringing me back as a speaker at their next conference and, to my surprise, they said yes. I asked them why. After all, I hadn't done very well.

Here is what the owner of the conference company told me.

"We'll bring you back because they liked you. That's 90% of being successful as a speaker. If they don't like you, it doesn't matter how good your presentation is. If they do like you, they'll forgive you almost anything."

I went on to speak at dozens more of their events and, I'm happy to say, my presentation improved considerably.

But what he told me has always stuck. I think that was a great insight.

They took that likeability factor seriously. While they asked every attendee to complete a detailed feedback form, they also had people sitting at each side of the room, looking at members of the audience during each presentation. The feedback forms gave them some valuable information. The people watching the audience and studying the attendee's body language then came back and told the organizer whether the audience liked the speaker or not.

I have used that lesson while writing my own websites. For my coffee sites I can't compete with Starbucks when it comes to authority and brand awareness, but I can write in a way that makes my readers like me more than they like Starbucks.

This curves back around to the concept of the expert next door.

Remember how we were going to ask our neighbor about the problems we were having with our roses? Yes, we could go to the local nursery and find an expert. But we might suspect that his or her opinion could be tainted by the desire to sell more roses. So maybe we'll ask our neighbor, because he has fantastic roses.

What's the major factor that will determine whether or not we ask our neighbor? We'll decide based on whether or not we like him. If we don't like him, we won't ask, even if we suspect his advice could be really excellent. If we do like him, we'll definitely ask, even if we think his expertise isn't exactly top of the line.

The likeable expert next door has empathy, which we talked about earlier. Empathetic people are likeable because they care about you. They are not aloof, they don't hold themselves above you in some way, as superior to you and as separate from you. An empathic, likeable expert next door knows what it is like to be you. He or she listens, wants to help, and wants you to succeed and be happy.

Big media and big corporations are not empathetic, almost by definition. Their contrived empathy is false, driven by their urgent desire to get their hands on some of your money.

As for you, as an individual working on your own website, you can and should be empathetic. Your readers will like you as a result. And if they like you, they will want to read what you write.

Five things to think about when writing as an empathetic, likeable expert next door.

Remember, the new path to riches model depends on finding and filling the gaps that big media and large companies don't or can't address successfully. Writing in a friendly and empathetic way represents one of those gaps. And it's a big one.

1. Write your website as if you were writing to a friend.

Too many people think they have to get serious and formal when they write. This is something we learned when were children at school and employees at work. First we wanted our parent's approval when we showed them what we had written. Then we wanted to impress our teachers. At college we were shown how to write in an academic style, which was necessary if we wanted to score highly on our papers and in our exams. When we started work, we had to learn how to write in a way that is appropriate for business.

The end result of all this *teaching* is that our own voices become muffled and hidden. We suppressed our own, natural ways of expressing ourselves in writing in order to win the approval of our parents, teachers, profs, and bosses. That's a pity, because all that training simply drains the personality out of our writing.

If your own voice and personal way of writing survived at all, it is probably best represented in how you write to your friends, in e-mail and elsewhere online.

It's that genuine, personal voice that you need to use for your website. Remember, you don't need anyone's permission any more. You don't need anyone's approval. You can and should just write naturally.

When I'm teaching writing for the Web I usually suggest that people imagine they are sitting at the kitchen table with a friend and explaining something to them. In my case, I might be answering a friend's question about the difference between various types of coffee makers. That's how I write. I write as if I were simply sharing what I know with a friend. My writing style isn't formal, nor does it sound like I'm writing for the benefit of a teacher or an editor. As the owner and writer of my own website I can write in any way I wish, without having to impress any higher authority. I choose to write in a friendly, accessible, and informal way, because that's what comes naturally to me.

2. <u>Write with the genuine empathy of a friend. Don't pretend to be a friend.</u>

Doubtless you have seen those e-mails that are personalized with your name and then gush enthusiastically, as if the writer were a close friend. They chat about how they have just been to the beach with some friends, had a great talk and then just had to rush home and write to you because the news they wanted to share was just so incredibly exciting. Well, that's nonsense. They are not your friends. They just want your money. They pretend to be your friends because they too understand the power of empathy. But their empathy is manipulative, it's not genuine. They are playing a game, because they know it will fill their bank accounts.

Don't do that with your website. Don't try to trick people by pretending to be what you are not.

When thousands of people come to my sites each week, they are not my friends, and I am not their friend. I don't even know who they are. And I don't pretend to be their friend. But I can still write to them in a voice and tone that is genuinely friendly. How do I do that? It's not a trick of writing style. I can do it because I genuinely do care about the experience people have on my websites, even if they are strangers. I do want them to find the information they are looking for. I do want them to get good advice and find themselves better informed.

It's the difference between pretending and simply being. I don't pretend to care about my readers, I do care about my readers. That simple distinction will have a profound effect on how you write. When you *pretend* to care, then you write like a professional, like a copywriter. It is your job to give an impression of caring. When you *actually* care, you simply write naturally, in the voice of that likeable expert next door.

3. Decide on your point of view.

What is your role? Are you an objective provider of information? Or are you an advocate, holding a clear and unmoving position? Are you an expert, or are you a beginner, just like your readers?

As the writer of CoffeeDetective.com I maintain a fairly objective and balanced viewpoint. I don't claim that if you want to make the best coffee you *have* to use a French press, and that all other coffee-making processes are inferior. Instead, I write about all the various ways to make coffee. I'll talk about the good and bad points of each.

From time to time I'll express a personal preference, because I do have some preferences. But even then I will usually include the other point of view. I position myself as the expert next door and might say, "Personally, I prefer X, but that doesn't mean you shouldn't check out Y and Z, and make up your own mind."

This approach works fine for me. It comes very naturally to me. It's how I am. It is always easy to maintain a consistent writing style when you base it on who you really are. And the more you share your true self with your readers, the more they will like you.

But my way isn't the only way. You can also write as an advocate, holding a very specific point of view. For instance, I could write a site that is only about Fair Trade coffee. I could make it clear that my personal belief is that everyone should buy only Fair Trade coffee. I could get heated under the collar about how coffee workers are treated, and demand that people support those workers by paying a few pennies extra for coffees that are Fair Trade approved.

That's a very legitimate point of view to take, and a strong basis for a really valuable website. Of course, it will work best if you really are an advocate and really do feel passionate about the subject.

When you write from this point of view you will almost always attract a smaller audience, but you can certainly build a much more passionate group of followers. In a way, you would be writing something like a fan site. Fan sites for a particular football team, for example, attract only those people who support that team, but they are passionate and engaged and full of energy.

There are other points of view you can take.

Are you an expert, a gifted amateur, or in the same position as your readers?

Here is how that works:

a) "I am a professional at making online videos and I will teach you everything you need to know."

b) "I used to be just like you. A few years ago I couldn't bake a cake to save my life. Now I make beautiful cakes every time, and I can show you how to do the same."

c) "I am just like you. I am a complete newbie at home decorating, but am about to redecorate my entire house. Follow me as I learn, and I'll share everything I get right...and wrong!"

The professional position is familiar to us all. It is the model used by big media.

The middle one, the expert next door, works very well online. There are thousands of successful sites like this.

The third one is interesting and very appealing to a lot of readers. People get fed up with being looked down on by experts and know-it-alls. They like the idea of following the struggles of an amateur and learning with them, side by side. It's comforting to know that other people share the same challenges. This approach is also ideally suited to interaction. Include a forum or blog, so your readers can write in and tell you about their own journeys.

4. <u>Find a way to invite and answer questions.</u>

The Web is an interactive medium. Take advantage of that. Allow and encourage your readers to interact. Your readers will like you for being open to their input.

My CoffeeDetecive.com website was transformed on the day I added a questions and answer function. People go to the Q&A page, write their questions in a form I have provided, and click on the submit button. I then answer the question and post the question and answer on a new page on the site.

This has worked well for me, and others, for a couple of reasons.

First, it shows I am not hiding behind my site, just creating content, regardless of the answer my readers are actually looking for. Instead, I step out front, make myself available, and acknowledge that my readers also have value to contribute. They like me for that.

Second, it gives me insights into what my readers really want to know and learn about. Yes, I can use various web-based tools to get a feel for which searches and questions are popular. But nothing is so direct, immediate, useful, and inviting to people than to write in with their questions.

Day by day, I get a better insight into what my readers really want. Not only am I answering questions, but I am also finding out new topics to write about, most of which I would never have thought of without the input of my readers.

My way of inviting my readers to contribute is not the only way. You can also use blogs, forums, surveys, polls, social media tools, and more.

Whatever route you take, try to find at least one way to listen to your readers. Listening is fundamental to any and every kind of relationship. Ask a marriage guidance therapist. She'll tell you that people are constantly upset about being shut out. "How come he/she never listens to me, or asks me what I want?"

The Web is interactive. People don't just want to read what you say, they also want to be heard.

Again, this is where you have a wonderful advantage over big media and big companies. The big guys never listen, and when they do their motives are clearly self-serving. They trot out the usual nonsense, like, "The better we know what you want, the better we'll be able to serve you." Yawn. As the writer of your own website you can take advantage of their weakness. You can truly listen to your readers, and be genuinely interested in what they say and ask.

5. <u>Be different, show some character.</u>

At kindergarten we are allowed to be different. After that, not so much. We are trained to follow the rules and color between the lines, without going over the edge. Same thing in high school, but with different rules. Same again with our first job, and the one after that.

I would encourage you to color over the line when you create your own website.

Show a little character, be interesting. Say things that other people don't say. Risk offending a few people.

Why? Because on the Web we really like people with character. We love the voice that stands out from the crowd. It's like going to a party at someone's house and finding there is someone really interesting there. Everyone else is saying the same old stuff, rehashing the same old topics, and more or less agreeing with one another. But that one person is different. He or she has different opinions, interesting points of view. What a relief.

If you want to stand out from the crowd online, it helps if you are different. You don't have to go crazy with this. Don't manufacture a difference for the sake of marketing and positioning your website. Just be yourself. Because when you let yourself go and stop behaving in the way you are supposed to behave, you *are* different. Give that part of yourself some space to shine.

What happens is that people really like to find someone who stands out from the crowd. And, because the Web is such a connected communications platform, those people who find you will tell other people. Your readers aren't going to rave about you on Facebook and Twitter if your site is the same as everyone else's. But they will if it's different.

What's your thing? Whatever it is, go for it.

Again, we have to take a look though those lenses we talked about in the last chapter. We have to find a gap where there is sufficient interest, but not too much quality competition. We have to make sure we can write plenty of pages about our topic. And so on.

Now we have another lens to consider.

Is this topic really your thing? Over the years I have come across numerous topic ideas that appear to have potential. But most of them I never looked into too deeply. How come? Because they were not my thing...or one of my things.

For instance, I might find an amazing, wide open niche in the area of organizing kids' birthday parties. But I wouldn't pursue it, because the topic really doesn't grab me. Or I might find a quality information gap in the area of natural health care for horses. Well, I don't have any horses.

It's true that you can quickly build up a body of knowledge in just about any area, just as I did with coffee. If you have a curious mind and like to learn, no area is really out of bounds. But you should still listen to your gut.

There are two things to consider here. If the topic doesn't feel like a natural fit for you, writing the website is going to be more like work, and less like fun. It will be a slog. When a topic interests you, learning is a pleasure. When it doesn't, learning feels like being in school, where you are required to learn about stuff you're not interested in.

More to the point, if the topic isn't your thing, and doesn't spark any interest for you, your readers will know it. The best writing always has some life and enthusiasm to it. I'm not talking about that false enthusiasm that some marketers employ, I'm talking about the real thing. When you do like your topic, genuinely, every page you write will have some extra life and energy. Readers love that, they love to feel the writer's natural enthusiasm shining through. Your readers will not only soak up that energy and like you for sharing it with them, but they will also feel more inclined to join in, whether by signing up for your newsletter, adding comments to your posts, or taking part in your forums.

Give your readers what they want.

Giving your readers what they want is not only a great way to get them to like you, but is also fundamental to the success of your website as a whole.

This is tricky. Because what people want is often not the same as what you think you should give them.

Let me give you some examples.

If you created a site about dating and relationships, you could create some great value for your readers by taking the position that finding a life partner is not something you can do in one weekend by going down to a singles bar. But, more often than not, that isn't what your audience wants to hear. What they want to hear is, "Here are 10 Killer Tactics That Will Attract the Partner of Your Dreams in Less Than 60 Minutes."

If you created a site about celebrities, you might want to write some in-depth bios of the stars, showing how they worked hard to get to where they are today. But, perhaps sadly, what most people really want is photos of movie stars looking terrible as they come out of their local supermarket.

There are two ways to deal with this disconnect between what you want to write and what your audience wants to know.

First, being fully aware of what you are doing, you can decide to target a smaller niche audience of people who really do want to learn interesting and useful information about your topic. Just take that path deliberately, knowing full well that you will be appealing to only a small fraction of the people who are interested in, for example, dating or movie stars.

Second, deliver your information in two stages. First, give them what they want and then say something like, "You know, there's a lot more going on beneath the surface of this topic. Stick with me and let's explore the depths together." In other words, you attract them to your site by giving them what they want, then you keep them coming back by giving them a deeper level of more interesting and useful information.

Whichever route you take, be sure that you remain aware of any disconnect between what you want to say and what your audience wants to hear. If you don't think this through, you can end up with very disappointing results and wonder what on earth went wrong.

When big publishers make this call, they are putting everything on the line when they publish a book or launch a magazine. Once the presses start running, there is no going back. More often than not, they take the safe route and just give people what they want. Hence all those magazines at the supermarket checkout showing photos of celebrities.

As a lone publisher of a website, working from home in your pajamas, you don't have to live or die based on a choice made on any particular day. You can always adjust and change your website. You can listen to reader feedback and update your homepage or some of your interior pages. You can get a sense of what people want. You can test two or more different approaches and see which one works best.

Finally, when you do get feedback, listen to it. If you get feedback through e-mails, comments, or survey results, be careful of that voice in your head that says, "My readers may want me to change X, Y, and Z, but I don't agree. That would spoil the whole site. That's not the direction I want to take."

If you find yourself responding to feedback in this way, ask yourself whether you are writing this website for yourself or for your audience. If you are writing for your audience, want to increase your traffic and want to make some money, you need to take notice of what your readers are asking for.

Being responsive and being willing to change a page or message within a few minutes is what separates you from big media. Big media can't change that book they just published. Companies and organizations are also very resistant to making changes quickly. It costs too much money, ties up too many resources, and upsets too many of the people who were involved in version number one.

Use this advantage. Make changes according to what your readers want. They'll like you for it.

You can't please all of your readers all of the time.

Being likeable and accessible is central to the success of your website. To be successful, you need to give people what they want. But that doesn't mean you should act on every single comment that comes your way.

If you change your homepage in a way that will please the majority of your readers, you'll probably hear back from one or two people who hate what you did. It's always like that. The only way to please everybody is to delight nobody. To avoid negative feedback from your site, you would have to descend to the lowest common denominator. You would have to be gray and boring.

Just figure out what *most* of your readers want and give it to them. If a handful of readers don't like what you are doing, let it go. Your task is to find the gap and then please the majority of the people within that gap. You can never please everyone.

CHAPTER SEVEN

HOW TO BUILD YOUR WEBSITE OR BLOG

Once you have an idea for your site and are ready to start writing and building, you will be faced with an interesting question—which tools or services are you going to use to actually design, host, build, and create your website?

If that sounds intimidating, don't worry.

The first thing to recognize is that building a website is a great deal easier than becoming a publisher in the offline world.

This is the heart and soul of what has changed with the Web. You are no longer confined by the process of creating and distributing physical publications. For a very simple website or blog you could go online now and have your homepage completed and published within a couple of hours. And it needn't cost you a penny. This is how the process of publication has become democratized. There are no longer any significant barriers to entry. Anyone can become a publisher.

That said, a hurriedly created homepage hosted for free is not going to lead you very far down the new path to riches.

Is creating and publishing your website expensive? No, it isn't. Certainly not when you compare it to the cost of offline publications, and not when compared to what your website can earn you.

As an example, my CoffeeDetective.com website generates revenues that average about $4,000 a month. That comes to almost $50,000 a year. And over the course of each year I spend about $400 on products and services to keep the site online and growing. Considering the size of the income I make with that one site, the costs are pretty modest. Of course, I also spend time on the site, but I don't count my time as an expense, because I do it as a hobby, and because I enjoy it. With this model, your major expense will be in time, not in cash.

Before we get into some of the details of choosing the best tools and services, let's look a little more closely at the issue of enjoying what you do when you write your site.

This shouldn't be like work. Don't create a second job yourself and dread the time you are going to have to spend on this. Find a topic that interests you, where learning will be as pleasurable as teaching others.

You'll be climbing a learning curve on the topic you choose, and you'll also be scaling a learning curve on the technology of creating and improving your website. There are different levels of learning you can set yourself, and if you are truly technophobic, there are options available that take no more skills than learning to use a simple piece of software, like a browser or word processing program. However, the more inquisitive and curious you are about the technology, and the more you are willing to learn, the more options you will have when developing and improving your website.

Here are three approaches to take, starting with the most complex and working our way down to the simplest.

1. <u>Learn to use Dreamweaver and create your website from scratch.</u>

MS Word is the dominant program for word processing. Photoshop is the dominant program for editing photographs and images. Dreamweaver is the dominant program for creating web pages.

As with most programs, you only have to learn about 20% of what Dreamweaver offers in order to achieve about 80% of what most users need. The toughest part is coding the original design and layout of your pages. What I do is get someone else to do that part. I describe what I want, draw a sketch, and then have someone code the first version of the page layout. Once I have that, I can simply copy and paste that same code for every other page I create. All I then have to do is write and insert the new content for that page. If you don't know anyone who can do that original coding work for you, you can easily find a freelancer on sites like Elance.com or Guru.com.

Once you have created or edited a page, you simply upload it to your hosting account with an FTP program.

All this takes time to learn, and Dreamweaver isn't inexpensive. But if you do take this route, you will have total control over your site.

2. <u>Use a Content Management System, also known as CMS.</u>

Aware that most people don't want to learn programs like Dreamweaver, companies have created all kinds of services to make the process of website creation a lot simpler.

Services like WordPress, Joomla, and Drupal allow you to choose a template, customize the look, feel, and functionality of your site and add your content through simple forms. They are becoming increasingly sophisticated in what they offer, and many of their customers' sites have a truly professional look.

The downside? Understanding these services and learning how to use them can be a struggle. These are professional grade services and take some figuring out. Once again, you can find a freelancer to do the setup part and to teach you how to use the tools to add your content. As soon as you get past the setup stage, it's smooth sailing.

3. <u>Use a service that has been designed specifically for home site builders like you.</u>

There is a whole different level of services which have been created for low-tech users. These work on the assumption that you know nothing about site building and are not much interested in advancing your technology skills.

These services include SiteBuildIt, SquareSpace, and Yola. These services, and others like them, make it as easy as possible for you to choose a site template and start building pages as quickly as possible. And when you do build pages, you'll simply be cutting and pasting text into forms. It is very simple.

If this is the level of service you feel would suit you best, do some research, staring with SiteBuildIt, SquareSpace, and Yola. Look at their pricing and the tools and functions they include for the price.

Two things you must watch out for.

When you use the easy-site-builder approach, there are a couple of things you need to watch out for.

First, be sure that the service or package you choose allows for an unlimited number of pages. Some services offer a very low price, but only if your site has a very limited number of pages. For example, you might find a website hosting package that costs $8 a month, but with a maximum of ten pages allowed. You need to pass on that. The new path to riches model is based on search engines listing dozens and then hundreds of pages on your site. So you need to choose a service and package that allows for unlimited pages.

Second, be sure that you have access to the source code for your entire site. Let me explain why. Let's say you start off with fairly modest ambitions and build your site with a service that doesn't allow for much in the way of expansion. Then, maybe a year or two later, your site is doing well and has outgrown the level of service you are receiving. At this point you may want to transfer you site to a different hosting service and package. For this, you need access to your source code. If the service you are considering doesn't make it clear whether or not it would be easy to transfer your site elsewhere at some future date, call them up and ask. It is worth spending the extra few minutes to make that call than to find yourself with nowhere to go a year or more down the road.

Make your choice based on what you know now, and also on what might happen in the future.

Consider options one through three carefully. I haven't listed them in order or preference or suitability. Choose the one that feels like the best fit for your level of technical knowledge. Option number three, while the simplest, can be more than sufficient for your needs. Indeed, CoffeeDetective.com is built and hosted on the SiteBuildIt platform. Other sites I own were created with Dreamweaver. And I have one site that uses WordPress. Different situations call for different solutions.

The key here is to choose a platform or service that isn't too expensive, but which does allow for you to keep growing and improving your website indefinitely.

Should you write a website or a blog?

Good question. Either option can work for the new paths to riches model. Let's spend a few moments looking at the difference between the two.

A website is made up of static, largely unchanging pages created within a structure that looks like a family tree, with the home page as the "parent". You can add pages and change pages, but the structure or architecture of the site will remain more or less the same.

This kind of structure allows you to write an indefinite number of site pages, and place each one in a relevant category. For instance, on my coffee site. I might have a page about a particular Bunn coffee maker, which is a "child" of my coffee maker category page, which is a child of my home page.

This kind of tree structure makes it easy for your readers to drill down to the information they are looking for. Someone might arrive at the home page of a site about garden ponds, quickly see the navigation link for aquatic plants and from that page find the topic that really interests them...floating aquatic plants.

The structure of a good website endures. It becomes familiar to your readers. They know where to find stuff. It's like being a regular at your local library and knowing exactly where the shelf is for murder mysteries. You have been there before and you know where everything is. It's familiar.

This static structure is common to most websites today and has a lot to be said for it.

Now let's look at blogs. Blogs are essentially journals. You write posts on a regular basis, and the latest post appears at the top of the page. A blog has one primary page, the home page. Hidden behind that is an architecture made up of various categories, which are similar to the second level page on a website. Indeed, some blogging platforms, notably WordPress, allow you to create static pages. Essentially you end up with a website that has a blog on the home page. You can do the same by building a traditional website and then adding a blog to the front page, as is the case with OneCupCoffeeReviews.com. That site started out at a regular website and then I added the blogging function to the home page.

Which approach should you take? A website or a blog? Whichever route you choose, don't make your decisions for the wrong reasons. I say this because many people choose blogging simply because it is easier to get started, and often free. For example, you can create a blog with Blogger or WordPress for free. But that isn't a good reason to choose blogging.

Where I use a blog it is because I have a topic that lends itself to fresh news. If you want to write about electronic gadgets, a blog can work well because your readers are always fascinated by what's new. They want the latest information. A blog is also great for opinion pieces, allowing you to follow one post with another.

As I said, either choice can work. But before you choose, consider the reason why most of my sites are exactly that, websites. And not blogs.

With a website I am creating a static body of information. I am also creating a passive source of income. If I am busy with other projects I can ignore one or all of my websites for weeks at a time. If I am away on vacation I can ignore those sites for all the time I am away. This, to me, is central to the whole concept of passive income. If my websites demand my daily attention, they would hardly be passive. It would be my new job to keep them regularly updated.

When you build your new path to riches around a blog, you lose one aspect of the idea of passive income. A blog is a journal and almost every really successful blog is added to on a daily basis during the week. You won't find many successful blogs that are updated less frequently than three or four times a week. In fact, when you go to a blog and find nothing new has been added for a week or so, you might be forgiven for thinking that the writer has given up. Having a blog that is not updated and added to regularly is like publishing a daily newspaper, but not bothering to print and distribute an issue for several days of the week.

So before you choose to write a blog, be sure that you are ready to make that level of commitment. Over the years I have started several blogs, with the best of intentions, and then found myself lagging behind. Some days and some weeks I am just too busy with other stuff to spend time on my money-making sites. That's no problem for my websites, but does become a problem for my blogs.

The trouble is, my early enthusiasm for the topic blinds me to the fact that there really are times when I won't have time to add new post several times a week. Then reality sets in and my blogs lose momentum, and the people who were following my posts drift away to other blogs where they can be more certain of receiving the fresh news and opinions they want.

Choose carefully, and then commit yourself.

My advice is that you write a website. And choose a service and a platform that allows you to grow and develop your site month by month, and year after year.

A website that generates a consistent and growing level of passive income is a site that doesn't stand still. For my own sites, I am constantly adding new pages and developing new ideas for different kinds of content.

My CoffeeDetective.com website started out simply as a collection of information pages. Then I added a page where people could submit their coffee photos. Then I added a page that allowed people to write in with questions. More recently I started creating and adding some videos on various aspects of making coffee. The site has been up for over three years now and I never stop thinking about how I can improve it, add to it, and make it more useful to my readers.

Build on a foundation that will allow you keep growing, developing, and improving your website for years to come.

CHAPTER EIGHT

HOW TO PROMOTE YOUR WEBSITE AND GET PLENTY OF VISITORS

Creating a great website filled with quality content is one thing, getting people to find it and read what you have written is quite another.

There are billions of web pages out there and, inevitably, some of them will be on the same topic you plan to write about.

In this chapter we'll talk about the specifics of getting your website known and linked to.

Remember, the new path to riches model focuses on getting free traffic. Yes, you can buy ads for your website if you want, but the cost of doing so will take a big bite out of your revenues each month.

Tap into the inquisitive and connected nature of the Web.

A billion people are on the Web worldwide. They are inquisitive and curious. They want to learn things, discover things, and interact with other people who share the same interests. This is the dynamic arena into which you are going to position your website. You want people to find your site because they are interested in what you say. You want inquisitive and engaged readers.

This means you need to get in front of these people. You want people to find links to your website in all the right places. Whoever you want to come to your site, you need to get in front of them where they are hanging out right now. And you need to get in front of them when they use a search engine to seek out results for a relevant word or phrase.

Here are six proven ways to get traffic coming to your website.

1. Through the major search engines, directories, and bookmarking sites.

2. Through inbound links from other websites and blogs.

3. Through forums, lists, and social media platforms like Facebook and Twitter.

4. Through e-newsletters.

5. Through multi-media.

6. Through offline publicity.

We'll look at these one at a time. But before we do, keep in mind that success comes rarely from any single one of these sources. A successful site draws traffic from all six.

1. Get your website found by the search engines.

You don't need to submit your website to the search engines. They will find it, but only if you create some links that point to your website. Once you have published your first pages, start adding links to your site in as many places as you can. You can start with using bookmarking sites like Delicious.com, social media sites like Facebook and any number of relevant forums.

As soon as Google finds your site, it will add it to its index.

But getting the search engines to find your website is the easy part. The next step is to get them to like your site, and rank it high up in their search results.

<u>Use keyword tools to determine the supply and demand for keywords and phrases.</u>

The subject of search engine optimization is a big one, and a complete set of instructions on how to go through the entire process in detail is outside the scope of this book. (But this is covered in detail in my how-to program at www.MoneyMakingWebsiteSuccess.com).

However, I do want to take you through an overview of the process, so you can see how it fits in with everything else I have been writing about.

The search engines produce a massive amount of data, tracking both the content of billions of pages on the Web and the number of times that people use particular terms and phrases in their search for information. Put another way, they are tracking supply and demand.

The supply figure relates to the number of pages online that Google decides are relevant to your search. For instance, if you search for the term *lawn seed*, Google will list over 4,150,000 results for the two-word phrase *lawn seed*, and the words *lawn* and *seed* individually. If you put quotation marks around your phrase and search for *"lawn seed"*—Google will return 105,000 results. In the latter case, it is searching only for the phrase and not for the component words. It is worth remembering to use those quotation marks, because without them you get a hugely inflated number of results and you could decide that a topic has too much competition when, in fact, it doesn't.

Now for the demand figure. You need to find out how many people out there are using the term *"lawn seed"* to find the information they are looking for. There are various tools available to help you do this, all of which access the data generated by the search engines. For the best of these tools you will have to pay. However, among Google's webmaster tools, they provide a tool that can give you a pretty good insight into the supply and demand issue.

It is called the Google AdWords Keyword Tool and can be found here:
https://adwords.google.com/select/KeywordToolExternal

This gives you a pretty good idea of the supply and demand of any given keyword or phrase. It isn't perfect for our purposes, because the demand side is calculated based not on the number of organic searches conducted through Google, but from the number of companies and individuals who are bidding on that phrase through Google's AdWords service.

If you get serious about writing a site that has the potential to make you a good revenue, I would recommend that you invest in a more complete keyword search service like Wordtracker.com or KeywordDiscovery.com. Also, some Web hosting and creation platforms, like SiteBuildIt.com, include their own keyword research tools.

Whichever tool or tools you use, your task is to find relevant phrases with a reasonably high demand – lots of people use them when searching for information on your topic. At the same time, you want that phrase to have a relatively low level of supply – which means not many websites are addressing the subject of that phrase with quality content.

Always remind yourself why you are doing keyword research.

It is tempting to get hopelessly tied up in keyword research and become obsessed with finding the very best keywords. This is not a good thing. Always remember that your primary task is to write for your readers. You are working to impress and delight the people who come to your site. Smart keyword research is something you do in the background. It can certainly help you get more traffic.

But you should also remember that keyword research isn't just about getting higher listings on Google. It is also about hearing the words of your visitors. You might think that a particular widget should be described in a particular way. But a little keyword research could show you that people looking for information on that widget usually describe it in a different way. When that happens, change the way you describe it on your site. Listen to your readers, understand the language they use, and then write and edit accordingly.

Add your site to some directories.

Search engines are based on software. Lines of code determine where your site is ranked within search results. Directory listings are more commonly based on the choices of human editors. For instance, if you submit your site to Dmoz.org, your site won't be listed automatically. A human editor will check out your submission and website, and then decide on whether or not it is of a quality to include in their listings.

Dmoz.org is free, but there are other major directories which charge a fee. The Yahoo! Directory offers a free listing option, but don't hold your breath. If you want to be considered for their directory, and stand a good chance of being included, it will cost you $299.

Then come the mid-level directories like Exactseek.com and Searchsite.com. Finally, there are also hundreds of smaller directories, some of which focus in specific niche areas.

Is it worth being listed in directories, especially if you have to pay for the privilege of even being considered? Sometimes. Directory listings may not result in a lot of direct traffic to your site, but they do provide links for the search engines to follow.

When choosing directories, try to get included within those which use human editors, like Dmoz.org and Yahoo! Directory. After that, keep looking for others which have human editors and which charge a fee of some kind. Google and the other search engines know that it's tough to get listed in Dmoz.org, and it will be impressed by those sites that are included. Your site then gets extra brownie points in Google's view, and that will help lift all your pages in their search result listings.

Avoid directories that are a free-for-all, with no human editors and no barriers to inclusion. These are a mess, including thousands and thousands of sites and will do you no good whatsoever.

Add you website, and new site pages, to bookmarking sites.

Bookmarking sites allow you to create lists of favorites outside of your browser's favorites tool. In other words, instead of just tagging a site or page as a favorite privately on your own computer, you bookmark those pages online on a site where others can find and browse your favorite sites and pages.

Some of the most popular bookmarking services include Delicious, Mixx, StumbleUpon, and Yahoo! Buzz.

While non-site-owners use these services to collect and share their favorite websites, you can use them to help publicize your own website. By including your own pages as favorites you are making those links visible both to the search engines and to people who have an interest in your topic.

Most of these services go beyond just allowing you to create static lists of web pages. For instance, with StumbleUpon you create a profile and have your own page of favorites, including web pages, photos, and videos, and then build a community of other people who share the same interests. The larger the number of people who like the sites and pages you list, the more often those pages will be shown to other StumbleUpon members.

With Mixx you can join and create groups and submit your favorites not only to your own page on the site, but also to the group pages.

If you write interesting articles or opinion pieces related to the topic of your site, you can submit those pages to sites like Reddit.com and Digg.com.

The idea here is to get links to your pages out there in as many places as possible. The links will help increase the number of people who learn about and visit your site.

2. Get more brownie points by having links to your site included on other quality and related sites.

Google judges the quality of your website not by what you write, but based on the kinds of sites that link to you. If your site about cold weather roses is linked to from Garden.com, Google will be mightily impressed and will credit your site with some extra gold stars.

When you are starting out, it will be tough to get links from other major sites within your topic area. But you should get started with link-building right away, even if your first few links are from other sites which are at the same stage of development as your own. The longer your site is up there, and the higher the quality of your content, the easier it will be to get more established and popular sites to link to you.

How do you get these links? Get social with other site owners and managers. Don't bulk e-mail requests for reciprocal links. That's just annoying. Be real and correspond with other webmasters. E-mail them and introduce yourself. Keep in touch via Twitter. And so on. Once you have established a relationship, suggest a reciprocal link, where you both link to each other's sites.

Reciprocal links are fine. But even better is when you get a link from a quality site which you may not even know about. Why would they link to you if you didn't even know the people behind the site? One reason. They love your content.

As with so many other aspects of succeeding with your website, inbound links appear a lot faster when you have great information on your site. When you have five-star content, other webmasters and bloggers will link to your pages because your content will be recognized as being of value to their own readers. These links are uninvited, but very valuable. It is great to get surprise links coming in from people's blogs, Facebook pages, and so on.

The golden rule is simply to make your content interesting enough to be worth linking to.

And remember, quality inbound links are the number one way to let Google know just how good your site is. As a result, link-building is on the must-do list of everyone with a website. Without building quality inbound links you will be severely limiting your success.

3. Take part in forums, lists, and on social media sites like Facebook and Twitter.

As an individual you have a big advantage over corporations when it comes to the Web. You can get social without being overtly commercial about it. You're not compromised by your need to sell products or services. You are simply a provider of quality information. Interact, be helpful, and share your knowledge freely.

A billion people out there are connecting and interacting online on a regular basis. A slice of those people will be interested in your topic. They would like to know about your site and would like to learn from you.

As soon as your website is online, find forums, lists, and blogs which are related to your subject. Then dive in and take part. Leave comments on blogs, take part in forum discussions, subscribe to e-mail lists.

The idea here is not to use these places to blatantly promote your site. The idea is to become a helpful and valued member of a variety of related online communities. The more value you contribute, the more people will respect you. And they will click on links within your profile and signature files to check out your website. Then they may start recommending your site and linking to it.

Don't push. Don't aggressively promote your site. Just add genuine value to every community you join, and the traffic and links will follow.

Social media platforms have hugely accelerated the growth of online interaction. Create a Facebook page as a way to keep your readers and friends up to date with changes to your website. Find new friends who share your interest. Find out about their friends. Use Facebook tools and widgets to add value to your page.

Twitter is wonderful because it all happens in real time. It's happening right now, in 140 characters or less per Tweet. Use the Twitter search tools to find other people who share an interest in your topic and start following them. Again, add as much value to the conversation as you can. Twitter is a great way not only to get in front of people who might want to learn from your site, but also to meet your peers, other publishers with their own websites, and businesses.

Any tool, platform, or service that helps keep you connected is of extraordinary value to you as the writer of a website. Participating online doesn't cost you anything other than your time, and it can quickly expand the base of people who know about your site.

Don't skimp in this area. Getting social and connecting with others is a key component of the new path to riches model.

4. Publish a regular e-newsletter.

On many sites you will find an invitation to sign up for their e-newsletter. You will often be offered a free download as a reward for signing up. Do the same with your site.

Some would say that the growth of social media has eclipsed the need to write an e-newsletter. In part, that is true. People get weary of the flood of e-mails and e-newsletters that arrive in their inbox each day and would rather spend their time on Facebook, YouTube, or Twitter.

Once again, this is a reason to write a *quality* e-newsletter. If your newsletter is good enough and interesting enough, then people will sign up and read every issue.

Why bother? Because subscribers to your e-newsletter are far more deeply engaged with you that a follower on Twitter, for example. On social media, people's attention is fleeting. They have plenty of other people to interact with and follow.

But when you build up an engaged readership with an e-newsletter, you are building a tribe of fans who will always engage with you and are more likely to write about your site and tell their friends about it.

A good e-newsletter, written well, builds a deeper level of engagement. There is a lot of value there.

5. Reach your audience through multi-media.

The Web isn't about text alone. People also love to watch videos and look at images. They like to listen too.

Once your site is up and running, think about how you can include photos, videos, and audio. The inclusion of these elements will add value to your site, and will also enable you to reach new readers through some very popular websites.

As an example, soon after uploading the first set of pages of CoffeeDetective.com, I started take coffee-related photos. As a result, I had a whole new section for my website with plenty of photos for people to enjoy. I also invited my readers to submit their own photos.

There are a couple of important benefits here. First, Google Image Search can be a big source of traffic. Images on websites come with what is called an Alt tag. The Alt tag isn't visible on the website itself, it is part of the underlying code of the page. You use this tag to write a short description of the photo. You can't see it, but Google can. If you upload a lot of different photos, and use some relevant keywords and phrases in their Alt tags, Google will find and list those images.

In addition to driving more direct search traffic to your website, your photos and images can help you grow the number of people who know about you, and increase the number of inbound links. For instance, as well as adding photos to my coffee site, I also add them to Flickr.com. People find my photos on Flickr, discover who I am, and click on the link to my site.

Now for videos. When explaining the difference between two coffee makers, or instructing someone on how to make coffee, a video can often do the job better than text alone. So I have been shooting a library of videos which I then add to my coffee site. The videos are helpful to my readers and make the site, as a whole, more interesting and informative. They also give Google another reason to send me visitors. Google knows that people like videos.

As with the photos, I do more than simply host videos on my own site. I also upload some of them to places like YouTube, Yahoo! Video, and Videojug. Once again, I am creating new links to my site and also reaching a broader audience of coffee lovers who have never heard of my site before.

You can do the same with audio, creating instructional recordings or Podcasts. If you record podcasts, add them to iTunes and you'll be found by a large group of prospective visitors.

The nature of how people use the Web, particularly across multiple media, gives you the opportunity to improve your site, attract more search engine traffic, and reach people you wouldn't have touched through other channels.

6. Reach new prospects through offline media.

While it makes sense to reach out online in as many ways as possible, don't forget to consider some traditional, offline ways to promote your site.

Think about your local media. Take a look at local and regional newspapers, radio stations, and TV. All of them are looking for stories.

As an example, let's say your website is on the topic of green living. Once your site has a good number of pages and can reasonably be presented as a useful source of information on the green, ecological lifestyle, send out a press release to local media. Tell them what you are doing and that you are available for interviews. Also, present yourself as an expert in that area and let them know they can reach you for comments at any time they find themselves covering a related news story.

Journalists are constantly looking for stories and for people to interview.

Another way to reach out to them is in response to a story they have just covered. Let's say a local paper is writing about a proposed landfill and quotes something from a local government spokesperson. If you disagree with that statement, or have something to add, contact the newspaper and let them know.

And you don't have to confine your ambitions to local media. Back in the late nineties I launched a website with a couple of friends and pitched it to The New York Times.

The next week we were on the front page of their business section, including a screenshot of our site. As you can imagine, we saw a huge surge in traffic that day. It is undoubtedly a lot harder to achieve that today than it was back then, but don't discount big media altogether. Find the right time and the right story, and then make your pitch.

Never stop promoting your website.

Too many people think that the process of publicizing a website involves a flurry of activity at the time of launch, followed by silence.

Not so. The promotion of your site should never cease or slow down. It must be an ongoing, continuous process. Think of your website as a living entity, surviving within a growing, connected ecosystem called the Web.

While the new path to riches model allows for some breaks and pauses in the creation of new website content, it isn't so forgiving if you decide to sit back and stop promoting your site. For my own sites I probably spend 50% of my time creating new content and 50% of my time promoting the site.

This isn't promotion in the sense of old-style marketing. I'm not pushing my site or paying for advertising. But I am making sure that my site, and links to my site, appear in as many relevant places as possible. You don't know where your next group of readers might be lurking. You could have a group of potential fans who have never heard of your site. In fact, you can count on it being certain that there are thousands of people out there who would like your site.

Yes, these potential fans might find you through a search engine. But that isn't the only way they can hear about you. Think about those directories and bookmarking sites or Mixx groups or Digg stories or a local newspaper or a cable TV station.

Best of all are those times when you come to the attention of someone who also has a website, blog, or a ton of friends on Facebook. They not only find your site, but also tell others all about it.

Whatever your topic, there are hundreds if not thousands of forums, groups, social network sites, and Twitter followers who are interested. To get them to your website, you simply need to become a participant in the places where they already congregate.

Don't leave all the heavy lifting to Google. Google can be your friend and may well turn out to be your primary source of traffic, but you also want to tune into multiple communities of people who are already talking about your topic. Do that, and you are tapping into what the Web does best...which is to connect one person to another, one group of fans to another, one interest group to another.

The Web is a place where billions of connections are made every minute of every day. If you are not there, within that flow, you'll miss out on numerous opportunities to share your website and your writing. Join the flow, with energy and determination, and you'll be leveraging the power of social interactions online.

For most us, the alternative way of getting people to find our sites isn't very attractive. We don't feel that comfortable about writing sales letters, sales pages, and ads. We don't want to write pitches or indulge in hype and overblown promises.

If you want a lot of people coming to your site, these are your two choices. Either participate wherever you can online, or become a marketer. And if you do become a marketer, using slick language to persuade people to come to your site, be aware that every sales pitch you make has the potential to undermine the objectivity and perceived value of the content on your site.

When you invite people to your website, they arrive with an open mind. When you market your website, like a salesperson, people arrive with a certain level of suspicion and caution. Your content is already tainted by your visitors' reasonable suspicion that you are going to try to sell them something.

CHAPTER NINE

HOW TO MAKE MONEY FROM YOUR WEBSITE

Finally, the chapter you have been waiting for.

I have left this topic pretty much to the end simply because for you to succeed with this model, your focus on making money shouldn't overshadow the earlier stages of the site-building process.

All too often people upload half a dozen pages and then fill them immediately with ads. They are anxious to start making money and totally misunderstand the dynamics of building a money-making website.

If you publish a six-page website and then wait for Google to send you a ton of traffic within the first few days, you'll be very disappointed. It just won't happen. You need to write dozens of pages of valuable content. Then you need to keep working until you have a hundred pages, and then two hundred. And so on.

A website is like a net being cast into the sea and trawling for prospective visitors. A six square net will bring you in a very meagre catch. Visualize it. Imagine a fisherman throwing out a net that is three squares wide and two squares deep. How many fish do you think he will catch? Now imagine his net contains hundreds or even thousands of squares, wide and deep.

It's the same with a website. Visitors don't all enter through the home page, they enter through dozens of different pages. Each page is a square in the net.

Also, it takes time for Google to find, index, and start listing your website in its search results. Google and Bing may find and index your new website within a matter of days, if you create enough inbound links to the site. But that doesn't mean they will start sending you traffic right away. They won't. Google could index you today and you might get one or two visitors next week as a result. But it can be weeks and months before you start seeing a significant flow of search engine traffic. Google takes its own sweet time. It has to put you in the line-up of new sites and make up its mind about the value and quality of your site. When you first start appearing in its search results, your site might be on page twenty of the results. To get some of your pages listed on page one could take several weeks or months.

This is why you should never focus your attention on making money from your website during the first three months. Instead, you should be focusing on adding more and more pages of valuable content, and spending time on promoting your site through online communities, groups, and networks.

Here is another way to think about it. Imagine you are building a bricks and mortar store to sell shoes. You buy some land and start building the store itself. First the foundations, then the walls, then the roof, and so on. At what point are you going to start trying to sell shoes? While the builders are working on the foundations? As soon as the roof is built? Of course not. You are going to wait until your shoe store is completed and then you will finally open the doors to your customers. A website isn't exactly the same, because the "building" is never completed, you are always adding new pages. But you certainly can't expect a flood of visitors and money when you are just in the early stages of constructing the website.

Only when you have a solid body of content and a good flow of traffic should you start working on ways to make money.

There are two ways to monetize your site that are ideally suited to the new path to riches model.

What do I mean by "ideally suited"? I mean that for a monetization method to fit well with your information website, it should allow you to make an income without undermining your position as an authoritative source of quality information. You don't want your visitors wondering whether you are truly trying to be helpful, or are just trying to pitch someone's products or services.

In other words, you need to present yourself as the expert next door, not the salesperson next door.

Fortunately, there are two very effective ways to make money from your website that don't involve that shift from being an expert to being a salesperson.

1. <u>Contextual ads.</u>

The contextual ads you see most often on content-based websites are AdSense text ads from Google.

What does contextual mean? It means that Google's software will automatically deliver ads which are relevant to the content of your individual pages. If on one page you are writing about home exercise equipment, Google will place ads on your page which are for companies offering products and services related to home exercise equipment. If you have another page on healthy eating tips, Google will show different ads, directly related to healthy eating.

For your part, you just place a piece of code on each page. Google then looks at that page and figures out the best match between your content and its own inventory of advertisers and ads.

When a reader comes to your page and reads your article about home exercise equipment, they are probably quite close to the moment when they are going to actually buy something. The AdSense ads serve a useful purpose, because they present a list of companies which offer exactly the type of equipment your readers are interested in.

In this way contextual ads can add value to a page. You provide useful, editorial information, and the ads help take readers forward to the vendors who sell products and services related to what you're writing about. And each time someone clicks on one of those ads, you and Google share the revenue. Depending on the topic, and how much the advertiser is paying per click, you might make two cents, 50 cents or a dollar or more.

For the purposes of maintaining your position as the expert next door, contextual ads are the perfect fit. The fact that these are principally text ads, and are related to the content of your page, makes them less intrusive and a lot more relevant than most advertising. As a result, your pages don't look or feel as if they are there simply as a platform for the ads. The integrity of your content is preserved, but you can still make some money from those clicks. And if you have hundreds of pages and you have one or more blocks of AdSense ads on each page, those clicks can result in a significant income.

Something else to understand about the contextual ads delivered by Google and other companies is that they have utterly transformed the landscape for small publishers of content online. Before Google came along with AdSense ads, it was a real struggle for small site owners to make any kind of advertising revenues. First, most companies would look down their noses at small websites and simple not deal with them. The advertising networks, which represented many different advertisers, were no better. If you didn't have massive traffic numbers they couldn't be bothered even to talk with you. And if you did find an advertiser, you would end up displaying the same ad on every page. The ads may have been relevant to your site topic as a whole, but they couldn't drill down and be relevant to the specific topics covered on individual pages.

With the launch of AdSense small publishers were finally given a fair shake at making some money from their content. Today, it doesn't matter whether you are CNN or an individual writing a website about dog grooming, you can both add AdSense code to your pages and attract the same body of advertisers.

In the early stages of the life of your website you probably won't make a great deal of money this way, simply because you won't have enough pages to deliver a large enough number of ad exposures. But you can make some money right from the start, and that revenue will grow as your website grows.

2. Affiliate programs.

Being an affiliate means you are entering into a partnership with a merchant who sells products or services. The merchant pays you an agreed commission each time someone clicks through from a coded link on your site to the merchant's site, and then makes a purchase.

As an example, you might sign up for Amazon's Associates program and then add links on a page you have written about baking cakes. Let's say you add a link to a good food processor that is available at Amazon. Depending on how well you do with Amazon, they have a sliding scale, you can make anywhere from 4% to 15% of each sale that results from someone clicking through from the link on your page.

Whatever the topic of your site, there will likely be some relevant affiliate programs you can sign up for. Some will yield just a dollar or two per sale referred. Others can net you hundreds of dollars per sale. How much you make will depend a great deal on the cost of the product or service being offered, and the margin available to the merchant. For instance, merchants selling consumer electronics have only a very small margin to share with their affiliates. But merchants selling high-priced reports or guides, available as downloads, have sufficient margins to offer you 50% of the sale or even more.

As with contextual ads, affiliate links on your website can add value without disturbing the editorial flavor of the page. For instance, I might write a page about French press coffee makers and, within the body of the text, include an affiliate link to the French presses they have available at Amazon.com. It makes sense. My readers want to know about the French press method of making coffee. I write about it and also give them a link to place where they can buy a French press if they want one now.

With affiliate links I'm not trying to make a sale. I don't have to shift my language from being helpful to being promotional. The body and tone of the content remains the same. All I am doing is saying, in effect, "By the way, if you would like to see a range of different French presses and maybe buy one, click here." If they do buy one, I make a commission on the sale.

That's how I do it. With a light touch. I retain the integrity of my content. I maintain my position as the expert next door. This dovetails perfectly with the new path to riches model. Certainly there are affiliate marketers out there who are much more aggressive. They do write sales pages and do strongly encourage people to click on the affiliate link and buy right now.

Some affiliate marketers push too hard, and Google doesn't like it. In particular, Google recognizes and doesn't like pages which are very light on useful content and are clearly created simply to get people to click on an affiliate link to a merchant site. Google values quality, original content. As do readers. So affiliate marketers who have been creating pages for which the principal purpose is to get visitors to click on affiliate links as quickly as possible are now finding that Google is dropping those pages from its index.

Google is an advocate for Web users, and you should be too.

Remix and prosper.

For many websites AdSense and affiliate marketing are not only the first but also the most profitable and enduring sources of revenue. In my experience, they are also the most consistent and dependable ways to make money.

But, as your website grows, other opportunities will present themselves.

For instance, after writing a hundred pages on the topic of baking cakes, you might find yourself with enough cake recipes to create and publish a cook book. You can publish this as a physical book or sell it as a download. Or if you have a site about landscaping urban gardens, you might find you have enough material to write a how-to guide or even shoot and publish a DVD.

And yes, the publishing of books and DVDs has changed utterly over recent years as well. It is now very simple to self-publish a physical book and make a lot more money than you would through a traditional publisher. It's also easy to create DVDs on most computers today, and there are companies out there which will produce, stock, and ship those DVDs for you.

Once you have a good number of pages on your website, step back and ask yourself whether there is some viable way to remix and republish some of your content in a different format. If there is, consider the best medium for your publication, create it, and then offer it for sale on your site.

Remember the sequence. First you create a large body of content and thousands of visitors. Do that and you don't have to do what most people are faced with when publishing, which is to find an audience and sell hard. If you build the audience first, then you will already have a tribe of fans who will be delighted to hear you are publishing a book, guide, or DVD.

Finally, don't sell out.

Some people follow the path I have described and then go overboard once they feel they have gathered together a large enough audience of prospects. They sell too hard and flood the content on their sites with promotions that are too aggressive and pervasive.

From the day you push too hard, you are spending your asset instead of building it. Your loyal readers won't much like the shift from expert next door to salesperson next door. New readers will recognize you for what you have become—a salesperson.

If you tread more carefully and offer links, products, and services more sparingly, you can retain the respect and attention of your existing audience and capture the same from your new readers.

With this model your site can grow and grow and grow. Your site becomes an asset with real value. It generates income on a monthly basis.

Don't kill the goose to get your hands on the golden egg. Look after the goose, so it can keep laying for many years to come.

CONCLUSION

If you now follow the path described in this book, I urge you to be realistic in your expectations.

The new path to riches model works, but it won't earn you tens of thousands of extra dollars overnight. This isn't a get rich quick scheme. The process takes time and plenty of hard work.

When you are persistent, and refuse to give up, you will see the money start to come in. And when that money starts to flow, it's the best kind of money you will ever earn. It comes in every month, and it doesn't stop coming in just because you take a two-week vacation.

How much? That depends. My CoffeeDetective.com website brings in an average of over $4,000 a month. That's a nice second income. But I have other websites that bring in a lot less than that. Some make me only $500 a month. And I know other people who apply a lot more time and energy to this model and make tens of thousands a month. There are numerous factors involved in determining how much money your site will earn. But by far the biggest factor is the amount of time and effort you put into your site.

A few words about bogus promises to get rich quick.

Illusion is a powerful force in our lives, in almost every way. Put simply, we find illusion to be a lot more attractive than real life.

We buy into the illusion that purchasing a particular brand of jeans will make us more attractive to the opposite sex.

We buy into the illusion that drinking a juice made from some exotic Chinese herb will help us lose ten pounds.

Consider the lottery. Multi-million lottery prizes are won by regular people, people just like you and me. The marketers who promote lotteries want us to aspire to the kind of lifestyle the big winners can now afford. They sell us the illusion that if it can happen to the person who just won, it can happen to us. As with all illusions, there is an element of truth in that they say. We could become a big winner. The trouble is, the odds are not in our favor. In fact, the odds of our winning a multi-million dollar lottery prize are minuscule.

Now consider the illusions that are pitched to you online, the get-rich-quick schemes. Become a millionaire by next Tuesday!

Marketers tell you that if you follow their simple, step-by-step guides, you could become an Internet millionaire. To reinforce the message, they take photos or videos of themselves in their expensive cars, parked in front of their huge mansions.

We want to believe them. That's what makes an illusion so powerful. It is almost irresistible. We want to win the lottery. We want to lose weight. We want to be attractive to the opposite sex. And we want to find an easy way to make a lot of money.

One of the tricks online marketers use is to say something like, "If I can do this, anyone can."

Not true. It's a lie. We don't want it to be a lie, but it is. Just because someone goes from zero to millions of dollars inside a year doesn't mean the same thing will happen to you. There are so many variables within our lives. So many differences between the guy who did that and you or me. Our paths can never be identical to his, even if we take the exact same steps. He may have skill sets you and I don't possess. He may have met someone who turned out to be the perfect partner for his venture. He may have phoned someone who could help him with part of his plan at the exact moment when that person was receptive to the idea. We can never replicate the exact circumstances of someone's success. If we could, we would all be rich.

Yes, people spend a lot of money on get-rich-schemes. And that money is almost always wasted. The power of the illusion got them as far as buying the study course, DVD set, or audio guide. But then it all stops. Many buyers don't even open the package when it's delivered to their doors. What they bought was the illusion.

So what makes the new path to riches model so different?

The new path to riches model fits perfectly within the natural ecology of the Web.

It's not about selling, nor is it about pitching some too-good-to-be-true product or service. It is about fitting in precisely with what people do online. And what people do is look for answers to their questions. They search billions of times a day, looking for information and advice, news and opinions.

This model isn't about trying to make people do something or buy something. It's not about pushing or persuading. You don't have to create a market or a need. It's about tapping into what people already want, what they are already searching for.

The opportunity is real, because people use the Web to find answers to questions within very narrow slices. Thanks to Google and the other search engines, it is now possible to find information on even the most specialized topics. Address one of those topics and Google with find you and send relevant traffic to your site.

The time is right because big media companies are stumbling. Their structures and business models are not well suited to an environment in which they no longer determine which information is published. They are no longer the gatekeepers of the information we have access to. Nor are they able to effectively address narrow niches with relatively small audiences.

The expert next door is perfectly positioned to write about topics in ways that are empathetic, authentic, and real. We grow tired of the slick presentation of information being packaged and marketed by large companies. We are suspicious of their motives. They are tainted. We would rather learn from gifted amateurs who are truly passionate about their areas of interest and expertise.

The new path to riches model works perfectly within social media, where billions of one-to-one conversations and connections take place every day. Companies don't belong within social media. They don't use it the way we do. Their motives are suspect. But as the writer of your own website, you very much belong within the world of social media. It's the perfect way to reach out to find people who share your passions and interests.

This is a time where large publishers are struggling. But their struggle is your opportunity. Where they struggle and move sluggishly forward, spending millions of dollars in search of answers they won't find, you can be light on your feet, find gaps they fail to address, and reach out quickly to a grateful and enthusiastic audience.

Unlike big media, you don't need millions of visitors in order to pay the bills. Your costs are minimal. And you get to keep almost all the income you make.

The combination of the democratization of publishing and the simplicity of publishing online is opening up a new world of opportunity for writers and small publishers.

You can start creating your website with tools and services that are available online right now. The costs are minimal. As your website grows, you can add more and more content and functionality, including photos, videos, podcasts, and more.

To start, you first need to create a list of topics about which you are genuinely interested. You don't need to be a professional, nor do you need any qualifications. You simply need to write about what you know, and write in the way your neighbor would speak to you when talking about his or her wonderful roses.

Then you need to find a gap. Find that slice of your overall topic that is not being well addressed by other websites. Find a niche where there is a reasonable demand for information, but for which there is not too much in the way of quality information available on the Web right now. Go back to Chapter Five and remind yourself of all the different ways in which you can find that gap.

Once you get started, keep going. Don't give up. Be persistent. This model takes time. You won't get rich quick. Your traffic will build slowly. Your income from the site will be very small in the early days.

But the harder you work on writing your site and letting other people know about it, the better you will do. Over time you will find that the income from your site is beginning to make a difference in your life.

First, that income will be enough to pay your phone bill for the month. Then you'll find it will pay your phone bill plus your car payments. Then it will pay those bills, plus your rent or mortgage. At that point you'll look at your website not only as an enjoyable way to spend some time, but also as a significant source of income.

Is this process guaranteed to work? Yes and no.

The model itself certainly does work. But success is not automatic. I have started websites that didn't live up to my expectations. How come? In some cases I allowed my enthusiasm for a topic to blind me to the fact that there wasn't much of a gap for me to fill. Other sites have done poorly because I haven't given them sufficient attention or worked hard enough to consistently add fresh content.

This model requires plenty of work and plenty of patience. Once you have found a genuine gap, what remains is the will to keep working on the site and adding new pages. Yes, it's hard work. But it's work you can do at the times of your own choosing. There is no fixed schedule. You have no boss. Put aside an hour or two a day during the early months. As your site grows, you can cut back on the time you spend. But only if you want to. To succeed faster and do better, spend more time on your site and grow it faster.

When you get it right and your website starts to deliver a very welcome addition to you monthly income, you'll quickly come to love this extra revenue as it flows into your bank account. It is an income that is consistent. It is an income that is passive. By that I mean you can stop work on the site for a month or two and see no loss in what you earn.

And, unlike those get-rich-quick scams, this model gives you a source of income that is long-term. You don't have to start something new every month. You just keep improving your site and then watch the income flow in month by month, and year after year.

NEXT STEPS

Are you ready to get started on your own money-making website?

Do you like the idea of creating a website of your own that generates a healthy monthly income?

If you do, you'll want to get started.

For anyone who is already familiar with the Web and building websites, this book should be sufficient to get you started. You know how to build a website. You know your way around the various keyword research tools and services. Just go for it. Find that gap and fill it with great content.

If you don't yet have any site-building skills, and don't know how to get started, all is not lost. You can purchase a copy of my "how to" version of this book. It is a program called *How to Write Your Own Money-Making Websites*.

The program is about 300 pages in length and takes you through the entire process in a lot more detail. I wrote it so it would work even for people who have no experience using online tools or building websites. It's for you, for your neighbor, for your aunt, best friend, or teenage children.

Buy the program and take it page by page, step by step. You will be taught everything you need to know. Your purchase also includes ongoing support, including access to podcasts, teleconference calls and an active forum.

Find out more at:
www.MoneyMakingWebsiteSuccess.com

Nick Usborne
NewPathToRiches.com

Breinigsville, PA USA
18 November 2009
227772BV00005B/18/P